Easy ENTERTAINING

Easy ENTERTAINING

Bridget Jones

Special photography by James Duncan

ANNESS
PUBLISHING

Dedication
To Neill, my favourite party partner

This edition first published in 1995 by Ultimate Editions
an imprint of Anness Publishing Ltd
Boundary Row Studios
1 Boundary Row
London SE1 8HP

This book was previously published as part of a larger compendium,
The Complete Book of Parties, Celebrations and Special Occasions.

This edition exclusively
distributed in Canada by
Book Express, an imprint of
Raincoast Books Distribution Limited

Distributed in Australia by Reed Editions
Editorial Director: Joanna Lorenz
Project Editor: Jennifer Jones
Designer: Adrian Morris
Special photography: James Duncan
Stylist: Madeleine Brehaut
Home Economist: Sara Lewis
Illustrator: Kate Simunek

Typeset by MC Typeset Limited
Printed and bound in Singapore

PUBLISHER'S NOTE

All the projects in this book are easy and safe to make, but some general points should be remembered for safety and care of the environment.

❖ Always choose non-toxic materials whenever possible; for example, PVA, strong clear glue, and non-toxic varnishes.

❖ Craft knives, scissors and all cutting implements should be used with care. Children love to help making things, but should only be allowed to use sharp tools under supervision.

❖ Always use a cutting board or cutting mat to avoid damage to household surfaces (it is also safer to cut onto a firm, hard surface.)

❖ Protect surfaces from paint, glue and varnish splashes by laying down old sheets of paper or newspaper.

MEASUREMENTS

Every cook or craftsperson prefers to work in the measurements of their choice – whether metric, imperial or, where appropriate, cups. In this book the publishers have given all these different measurement systems. Remember, the golden rule is to choose one set of measurements throughout each project or recipe for accuracy and perfect results.

Contents

Entertaining with Ease

PERFECT PLANNING

*P*lanning is the cornerstone for success on every occasion, from the grandest of celebrations to the simplest of impromptu meals with friends. Thinking ahead about *unplanned socializing may seem to be a contradiction, but the clever host or hostess always has some suitable refreshment to offer and a few good ideas for adding a sparkle to an unexpected opportunity for entertaining. This section concentrates on both preparing for specific dates and receiving guests at a moment's notice.*

WHAT TYPE OF PARTY?

Deciding on the type of occasion is the obvious starting point for planning, yet it is not uncommon for what was originally intended to be a simple supper with friends to lumber ungracefully into becoming a more formal dinner or for a small buffet to evolve into a major party. Of course, both unplanned transitions may be extremely successful, but there is always the danger of unforeseen hitches or an oversight along the lines of communication which may spoil the guests' enjoyment or, more often, overtax the host and/or hostess. One of the classic sources of embarrassment to guests is turning up in the wrong style of dress, while the basic problem for a busy host or hostess is being overstretched at the last minute and neither spending sufficient time with the guests nor enjoying the party. Such occasions are always uncomfortable for everyone.

Many parties celebrate an event such as an annual feast, birthday, wedding, christening or anniversary; they can also take place for no special purpose at all other than to see friends. Whatever the occasion, it is most important to have a clear outline of the form of entertaining before beginning to work on any of the preparations.

Annual festivities, such as Thanksgiving, Christmas, New Year and Easter, often follow a traditional structure, but this does not free the host or hostess from planning ahead; it simply means that there are fewer decisions to make and that they all fall into an existing framework. For all other occasions, a decision on the type and size of celebration is the starting point and the usual pre-arranging has to follow. Begin by considering your likely budget, then clearly outline what sort of party you are planning within the financial restrictions. Work through the following points, and by the time you have made notes on these you will have a structure for planning all the details.

> ### Party Planning Checklist
>
> - **Time of day**
> - **Degree of formality**
> - **Dress**
> - **Numbers**
> - **Location**
> - **Food and drink**
> - **Invitations**

Time of Day

Is the event going to be breakfast or brunch, lunch, afternoon tea, cocktails or drinks before dinner, early supper, dinner, late supper, or drinks after dinner? If the party is linked to some outside event, check the exact timing for that. Wedding ceremonies and christenings are the obvious occasions, but the same applies to other likely opportunities for social gatherings – graduation, opening night at the local theatre group, a visit to the theatre, concerts, a sporting event and so on.

Degree of Formality

If you decide on a formal party, this will provide you with a set of clear-cut rules to follow. You may opt for complete informality, in which case you need to work out your own pattern of rules. However, many occasions fall somewhere between the two extremes. The important thing is to decide exactly how you want to entertain, let everyone know what to expect and stick to your decision by planning accordingly. Think in terms of dress, how you expect guests to participate and the type of refreshments, and pass all this information on to the guests.

The type of entertainment and refreshment must fit in with the level of party – delicate canapés or hors d'oeuvre are perfect for cocktails, but not when guests are dressed for a walk in the park followed by a hearty brunch; and coping with unsuitable food or boisterous indoor games is awkward when standing and chatting in evening dress.

The style of celebration will also dictate whether outside help is needed. Caterers, waiting staff and bar staff may be hired for formal occasions, such as weddings, and may also be employed for any large party or even for formal dinner parties. There are also several possibilities for commissioning outside entertainment on such occasions. These aspects of any party should always be planned at the outset, not as afterthoughts.

Dress

Formal invitations will always state whether morning dress, white tie (full evening dress) or black tie (evening dress) are required. If none of these options is specified when a formal invitation is dispatched for a dinner party, then men should wear lounge (dress) suits and women should dress up without wearing evening dress. Generally speaking, if you plan a dinner party for a group of acquaintances and friends, then the mode of dress should be good suits for men and smart dress for women unless you specifically request some other style. When inviting close friends to a dinner party, the dress code is usually understood within the group; however, take special care when inviting a mixture of close friends, who are aware of your style, together with acquaintances who do not know you well. On such occasions, simply make a decision and let everyone know what to expect.

Informal dress, on the other hand, invariably demands some qualification

because it can mean different things to different people. When invited to an informal supper party some men will dress in a shirt, tie, sports jacket and trousers, while others will put on jeans and a sweater; to women informal dress can mean anything from jeans and a sweater to a simple skirt and attractive shirt. The best way to deal with this is to let guests know what sort of clothes you intend wearing – and not to change your mind later!

The Guests

Bringing people together for dinner parties is not always easy and deciding on the group of people to invite to larger gatherings can be difficult. Nevertheless, this is an essential and important first step in good planning. If you organize a dinner party for people who are strangers to one another, it is important to mix individuals who are likely to get on well together or at least express an interest in one another.

When inviting friends to larger gatherings, always ensure that there are groups who will know or can relate to one another. Sadly, family, friends and colleagues do not always have much in common and, worse, the differences can split a poorly planned party. In a large party it is a mistake to invite just one or two people who are unlikely to socialize easily with the majority.

Think back over your own social experiences and you will probably recall occasions when certain guests in the minority have obviously lingered on the fringe of a gathering awaiting the first polite opportunity to take their leave. Having made the point, it is equally important to stress that there are exceptions and we have all witnessed outstanding social successes in the most unlikely groups of people.

Formal Dress

❖ Morning dress is worn for royal garden parties, Ascot and some similar events in Britain and other royal European countries, and at the request of the host and hostess at weddings all over the world. If you are planning a formal wedding, then make sure that all who are expected to wear morning dress are aware of the style which is being adopted. Black morning coat with striped trousers, grey tie and black top hat are traditional; however, there are variations on greys and blacks, as may be seen at any dress hire company. Women should wear hats to formal weddings, and *always* when morning dress is requested of the men.

❖ White tie is the traditional full evening dress, but it is now usually reserved only for grand balls and the most formal occasions. For the man, this means black tail coat, wing collar and white bow tie and black trousers, which usually have a double row of braid down the outside leg. Patent shoes are a traditional 'must', but not essential these days. Women should wear

long gowns on white tie occasions. Long white gloves may be worn with evening gowns, and these should come over the elbows.

❖ Black tie is the most common form of special dress for evening occasions and is simply referred to as evening dress. A black dinner suit (tuxedo) with white shirt and black bow tie is the conventional dress. A single-breasted suit may have a black waistcoat or a cummerbund; a double-breasted jacket is worn closed. There are many variations on this theme, with colourful waistcoats or cummerbunds and ties, even suits with various design details. However, many men do wear dark lounge (dress) suits with bow ties for evening wear. Women should wear evening dresses, which may be long or short.

A marquee (closed-sided party tent) in the garden is perfect for entertaining larger numbers at home.

Numbers

It is vital to make sure that you can cope with the numbers for the type of party planned. This is largely a matter of space. For example, it is not practical to arrange a formal dinner party for eight guests if you can only sit seven around the table: the eighth person who is perched on a stool at the corner of the table will make everyone else feel thoroughly uncomfortable. The same applies to a barbecue for fifty when the only grill is a small hibachi; a cosy kitchen brunch for ten in an area which is cramped with six people; or a children's party for twenty-five in a house which is overfilled when half-a-dozen children are invited and where there is only a small garden.

Remember that the equation can work the other way and that for some types of gatherings, success depends on having the party area fairly tightly packed with people. This applies particularly to hired premises, where the capacity of the room must be tailored to the number of guests expected – too few people in too large a space is false economy as well as fatal to creating any kind of party atmosphere.

Location

Decide whether your party is to take place indoors or outdoors, and whether you have sufficient space on home ground or should consider holding it elsewhere. For indoor entertaining at home, the main considerations are the room arrangements. Similarly, for outdoor events such as barbecues and parties in the garden on a modest scale, take a practical overview of patio space. Consider likely seating for those who require it, areas for children, the alternatives should the weather let the party down and so on. Think about hiring a large grill or two smaller barbecues, if necessary.

However, for larger gatherings and events such as large-scale garden parties and picnics, you may need to consider a separate location or a marquee (closed-sided party tent) or open tent.

TENTS AND MARQUEES Unless the house is suitable for entertaining with ease in large numbers, an open-sided tent or marquee (closed-sided party tent) is the practical option for home celebrations. You do not have to have a vast garden (yard), as marquees can be comparatively small; however, you must have a flat area where the tent can be erected. Look through the telephone directory for hire (rental) companies which cover your area and ask for details from as many as possible to give you an idea of price range and the facilities on offer. Depending on the time of day and the season, you may need power for lighting and some form of heating. Remember when hiring marquees to establish exactly what is included in the way of flooring and internal lining or trimmings. Establish details about erection costs, timing for dismantling and so on.

PREMISES When considering hiring (renting) a room, club house or hall locally, thoroughly check the rules and regulations which apply to the use of the premises. For example, is the place suitable for music and dancing, will it have a bar, is the consumption of alcohol allowed, is there a time by which the premises have to be vacated, and what parking arrangements are available nearby? Check the availability of kitchen facilities for any catering requirements. Make sure that you have access to the area beforehand for all your preparations and find out whether there are any additional costs.

The vital point to remember is that the location must be suitable for the occasion. This does *not* mean you have to hire only the grandest of rooms for formal functions, rather that whatever the surroundings, they live up to the event. For example, a modest church hall with dull furnishings – or a plain marquee (closed-sided party tent) – can be transformed with a little flair by clothing drab tables in linen and adding flowers and foliage. You also need to agree when any decorations can be put up and removed – if a location is heavily booked you may not have much time for such transformations – which you'll also have to schedule in to your timetable. When you make your initial enquiries, always discuss such details of what you hope to do and make sure they are acceptable to the owners. Apart from the risk of causing serious offence within small communities, you may discover that there are objections to some of your ideas when it is too late to change locations.

Pack a basket to picnic in style.

PICNICS Picnics may be arranged around an event at a pre-determined location, such as an outdoor concert, theatrical entertainment or parade. However, they can also be occasions for meeting friends or other families, in which case a suitable site must be found and checked out in advance of making definite arrangements. Try to visit the place beforehand at about the same time of day as the intended picnic if at all possible. What seems an idyllic location on one occasion may be quite different when busy with weekend dog-walkers or early-evening jogging enthusiasts if it is a popular spot.

Food and Drink
Whether the gathering is small or large, it is important to decide on the level of refreshments – nibbles (snacks), finger food, some form of buffet or a proper sit-down meal – and to make sure the food and drink are suited to the occasion. This must be considered alongside the time of day, numbers invited, budget and location, where appropriate. You can be quite individual in your choice of refreshments as long as they fulfil the requirements for the time of day and location and adapt well to the style of party.

The level of refreshment offered must also correspond to the expected length of the party. Light canapés or hors d'oeuvres may be served for a late morning or mid-day affair when guests are expected to depart fairly quickly, but if you anticipate entertaining for the whole of the afternoon, the range of canapés or hors d'oeuvres must be extensive and plentiful or more substantial refreshment should be offered.

Do not be afraid to make an unusual decision about the form of food, but do make sure it is adequate and that you can cope with the preparation or that caterers, if you are using them, do not need facilities which are not available.

Invitations
Whether printed, handwritten or extended by word of mouth, an invitation should convey certain important information clearly to the recipient. It should state the names of those invited, the name(s) of the host and/or hostess, the occasion and the reason for it, the place, the time and an address to which replies should be sent. Written invitations often include the formula "RSVP" in one corner, which stands for the French "*Répondez, s'il vous plaît*" ("Please reply"), to remind guests that an answer is required.

Where appropriate, an invitation will specify the expected time for guests to depart. For example, if you expect guests to leave a drinks party at a certain time, then state on the invitation "6–8 p.m.". This is a good way of emphasizing that the occasion is simply for drinks, and dinner or a buffet will not be provided. Any special form of dress should be detailed on the bottom of the invitation. Many invitations to casual parties also include the instruction "Bring a bottle".

TELEPHONE INVITATIONS These are appropriate for dinner parties, informal luncheons and supper engagements or for drinks with friends and for arrangements made at short notice. Telephone invitations to a dinner party are often a case of "setting a date" rather than inviting friends for a pre-fixed date. The length of notice varies according to the group of people, but it is usually within a period of two to four weeks, sometimes longer when fixing a date with busy friends. It is a good idea to follow up with a card to confirm the date and time when planning a formal dinner party, and to phone a day or so ahead of an informal event.

INVITATION CARDS Ready-made cards where you write in the details yourself are available in styles ranging from formal to fun. You can also arrange to have cards printed specifically for an occasion. As with dress, there are systems of etiquette that govern printed invitations issued for weddings and similar formal occasions, and it is important to consult a detailed reference source on the subject.

HANDWRITTEN INVITATIONS For smaller gatherings and less formal occasions such as dinner parties, beautifully scripted invitations handwritten on a well-chosen card or interesting paper are quite sophisticated. If you choose paper rather than cards, then try any of the handmade papers which are available from art shops and fold them neatly before writing on the front. Some have matching envelopes available. Look out for coloured inks or pens, particularly in gold or silver. It is best to plan the content and presentation of the handwritten cards carefully on rough paper first.

Christmas Star

This is the perfect invitation card to a Christmas party.

YOU WILL NEED: card (posterboard) for template, pencil, gold card, scissors, ribbon.

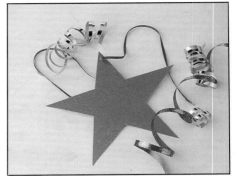

1 Scale up the template to the size required and transfer the pattern onto the gold card (posterboard).

2 Cut around the edges of the card using a pair of sharp scissors.

3 Make a hole in one of the points of the star using the tip of a scissor. Cut a length of ribbon and thread it through the hole so that it can be used as a decoration by the recipient.

A Masked Ball

An invitation in the form of a mask sets the theme for a fancy dress (costume) party. Make it life-size if you want to ensure that even the least creative of your guests will have no excuse for not coming in dress . Write the invitation on one side and decorate the edges of the invitation on the other side with beads, feathers and trimmings, if liked. Vary the decoration depending on the theme of the party.

YOU WILL NEED: card (posterboard) for template, pencil, thin coloured card, scissors, trimmings such as feathers and beads (optional), glue (if using trimmings), ribbon.

1 Scale up the template to the size required and transfer the pattern onto the coloured card (posterboard). Cut around the edges with a pair of scissors and cut out two holes for the eyes.

2 Decorate the edges of the invitation with feathers, if liked. Attach with glue.

3 Use a strong glue to stick decorative beads to the front of the mask, if liked. For a balanced effect, finish with a bead either side of a central cluster of beads.

4 Pierce a hole on each side of the mask using the point of a scissor and thread a piece of ribbon through each hole. Knot the ribbon at the front to hold in place. Pinch the central part of the mask to follow the shape of the nose.

Surprise Invite

Send this specially sealed invitation for a surprise party. The decorative seal in the centre can be adapted to suit the occasion, from a small rose made of silk fabric and attached with double-sided tape to a ready-made novelty self-adhesive paper shape depicting a fancy dress (costume) theme.

YOU WILL NEED: coloured paper, ready-made self-adhesive paper shape or sealing wax, ribbon (optional).

1 Fold a piece of coloured paper, 20 cm/8 in square, in four (the size of the square can be adjusted to match the size of your envelopes, if using). Open out the paper and fold the corners into the centre to form a smaller square envelope shape. Press the paper with a cool iron to eliminate the previous fold marks.

2 Write the invitation to the party inside the folds. Seal the four points where they meet in the centre with a self-adhesive paper shape or melted sealing wax.

3 If using sealing wax, the seal can be made more decorative with the addition of some ribbon. Cut two short pieces of ribbon and place them on the seal. Carefully melt a little more wax where the ribbons meet in the centre to hold them in place.

Stylish Hat

Novelty invitations are always popular. Make this stylish hat for an elegant summer party in the garden or for a romantic fancy dress (costume) party. Alternatively, design your own hat-with-a-theme invite to send out to guests. And there's no need to make the same hat for each guest — children in particular will love to receive their own special design.

YOU WILL NEED: card (posterboard) for the template, soft pencil, coloured card, scissors, range of coloured ribbons and ready-made bow in the shape of a rose, glue.

1 Scale up the template to the size required — check that the finished size will fit into your chosen envelopes. Transfer the pattern onto the coloured card (posterboard).

2 Cut around the edges with a pair of scissors. Cut a piece of ribbon to fit across the crown of the hat and stick in place. Cut lengths of coloured ribbons, fold in half and glue to one corner of the ribbon on the crown.

3 Stick a rose bow over the join.

4 Write the invitation details on the other side of the hat.

Don't forget to leave enough time for the finishing touches such as arranging flowers.

GETTING READY

Once you have decided on the event, set about organizing the preparations. There is the location to get ready as well as the catering to be done, and any entertainment must be planned. Make a realistic assessment of how much of the work you are going to undertake yourself, and how much help you are going to bring in from outside – in the form of practical assistance, friendly or paid. Apart from the question of food and drink, you will also need to consider what equipment may need to be bought, borrowed or hired.

Lists and a timetable are essential. Make a separate list for each aspect of the party planning: guests, shopping, household tasks, outside help, equipment hire and so on. Keep them all together in a folder. Prepare a programme of work for the week running up to a large party, with an especially detailed list of tasks for the day before and for the day itself. As each aspect is completed, tick it off the relevant list.

Catering Arrangements

Catering implies organizing the serving of food as well as its preparation. Catering companies will take the whole task off your hands, you can hand over some aspects to the professionals, or you can hire the services of individuals to prepare the food and help in other ways. Alternatively, you may decide to undertake all the catering at home.

Cooking at Home

It is very gratifying to be able to take the credit for having prepared a splendid meal yourself. Given good planning, it is possible for someone with the time and ability to organize quite a large spread from a domestic kitchen; other party-givers will find it more satisfying and relaxing to let someone else take the strain.

❖ If you intend dealing with the food yourself, be sure to plan a menu that you can prepare with confidence. Choose recipes that do not need too much last-minute attention. Take advantage of dishes that can be prepared ahead of time and frozen. Enlist practical help well in time, if necessary. Delegate friends and relations who are good cooks to make specific dishes. Alternatively, commission dishes from a freelance cook who may offer exactly the level of catering required to retain that 'best of home cooking' feel.

❖ Consider, too, the possibility of buying in a wide range of high-quality ready-prepared foods: smaller local delicatessens, for example, may be able to supply dishes if ordered in advance.

Equipment

As you compile your ingredients shopping list based on your chosen menu, make a checklist of any special cooking equipment you will need. Cooking pots and pans, such as cake tins or pans, cutlery (flatware), china and linen, for example, can all be hired.

A range of items can be hired for parties, including full sets of china.

Make a list of requirements and approach local companies for a quote (in Britain glasses can usually be borrowed free from a wine merchant with charges made only for breakages). As ever, it is important to establish exactly what you need, to determine the rates and to book ahead.

Preparing the Location

If you are hiring either a room or marquee, you are likely to have access to the place for only a limited amount of time before the event, and any de-

liveries or decorations should be scheduled into your timetable to take this into account. If you are holding a function at home, on the other hand, you may seem to have all the time in the world. It is all too easy to postpone paying any attention to the home itself, a mistake which can lead to extensive last-minute work just when you would like to devote time to the final details for the gathering. Think well ahead for large gatherings and make lists of things that have to be done.

CLEANING If you are hosting a formal function at home, then you may want the house thoroughly spring cleaned beforehand. This may be something for outside specialists to handle if you do not have a home help.

Fix the day for cleaning about five to seven days before the event, and even if you have a regular help, it is a good idea to suggest commissioning an outside agency to assist with heavy work. Make sure you have someone to freshen up all areas on the day before the party or early on the day.

DECORATIONS Allow yourself time to do the flower arrangements, and any more complicated projects such as swags or wreaths of flowers and foliage for formal gatherings. Even for

a small informal get-together, lay the table in good time to create a welcoming ambience for your guests.

Confirming Details

Finally, well ahead of time, make a checklist of vital last-minute points to confirm. This will probably mean telephoning to check details of orders placed, services commissioned, friends who have roles to play and guests that may need assistance in some way.

The Perfect Party-Giver

Always allow time for yourself, especially on important occasions when you have to front the whole show. You will be more efficient if you feel at your best, and more likely to enjoy yourself.

❖ Fix an appointment at the hairdresser's to have your hair cut or trimmed a week or so in advance. For a special party style, fix an appointment on the day.

❖ Decide what you are going to wear in plenty of time and make sure it is dry-cleaned or pressed if necessary and ready to put on.

❖ If you plan a facial, book it for a few days ahead (it can leave your skin looking blotchy on the day).

❖ Consider having a relaxing massage the day before, when plans are almost complete.

❖ Always allow plenty of time for

your personal preparations, including that essential soak in the bath or long, refreshing shower.

❖ Plan to be dressed, relaxed and sipping a cool, non-alcoholic drink 30 minutes before you expect the first guests to arrive.

MEMORABLE MENUS

The time and effort devoted to menu planning depends entirely on the type of party that you are organizing. At a dinner party, or similar meal-time gathering, the menu

and quality of the food is an important focal point, whereas some parties concentrate more on the entertainment and refreshments are kept simple.

Memorable menus fit in perfectly with the occasion and style of entertaining, from a breakfast spread to cocktail snacks or the grandest dinner party. This section sets out guidelines for planning refreshments to suit all occasions.

CREATING THE PERFECT MENU

The food must complement the event, whether it is the whole point of the occasion, one of several key features or a pleasing aside. Bear in mind the following general rules:

❖ The style of the menu must reflect the impression given on the invitation. For example, if you plan a celebration buffet, the food must live up to the occasion: bowls of nuts, crisps (chips), pretzels, some olives and a few salads will not do.

❖ Make sure the menu fulfils its intended role. If hungry guests are invited for a meal, don't palm them off with a snack. On the other hand, if you invite friends to a light lunch, it is equally inappropriate to serve them a hearty feast.

❖ Plan dishes that will be convenient to serve and eat in the circumstances of the party. For instance, avoid presenting guests at a stand-up buffet with food which really requires a knife and fork, a firm table and comfortable seat to be eaten neatly.

Special Diets

Dietary restrictions may be applied for health, religious or cultural reasons, or purely on the basis of personal preferences. If you invite acquaintances to a dinner party, the obligation falls on them to let you know of any significant dietary restrictions. It is always a good idea, however, when discussing an invitation over the telephone, to check with guests whether any foods are best avoided.

Religious dietary laws include the kosher rules which Jews follow; these are extremely complex, covering the whole process of food production and cooking, and many Jews no longer adhere to them strictly. However, pork and shellfish are not eaten, and dairy products – this includes milk, cream and yogurt – are not prepared or consumed with meat.

Muslims do not eat pork and they do not consume alcohol. Hindus do not eat beef or drink alcohol, and many Hindu sects follow a vegetarian or vegan diet. Buddhists are vegetarian.

These notes merely indicate certain restrictions that may apply. You will need to check with your guests (or with a well-informed third party) to find out exactly what is and is not acceptable.

A vegetarian diet excludes meat but usually allows dairy products such as eggs, milk and cheese. A vegan diet permits no animal products at all.

Providing vegetarian alternatives at a large buffet is easy. Egg and cheese dishes and salads of peas and beans such as chick peas (garbanzo beans) or green lentils are suitable for cold buffets, and vegetable gratins are ideal for hot buffets.

Menu planning takes a little extra effort when you invite one or two vegetarian guests to a very traditional dinner party. It is easy to prepare a vegetarian soup (remember to avoid animal stock) or other first course that everyone can enjoy. As a vegetarian main dish serve something like a ratatouille gratin, braised fennel with a gratin topping, stuffed courgettes or mushrooms, a terrine of celeriac (celery root) or vegetable couscous. Select the non-vegetarian dish next and choose other vegetable accompaniments that will go well with both main dishes.

❖ The taste, texture, colour and presentation of all dishes should be palatable and visually pleasing. These characteristics must be well balanced for each course and throughout the meal as a whole.

❖ If you are cooking the food yourself, consider your kitchen facilities and equipment, and plan a menu that will not overstretch either of these. Select dishes and quantities which you can prepare with reasonable confidence. Think about preparing some dishes ahead of time to freeze when cooking for larger gatherings.

❖ When catering for a large party or for people whom you don't know well, be prepared to accommodate some special dietary needs.

Formal Buffets

A buffet is practical for large gatherings, such as weddings and formal parties. The buffet may consist of hot or cold dishes, or a combination of the two. Canapés or hors d'oeuvres may be served beforehand. Ideally, the buffet should consist of a choice of fish, poultry and meat dishes accompanied by a range of salads and vegetables.

It is usual to serve one course, just the main course – no starter (appetizer) – at a buffet, followed by dessert and perhaps cheese; however, an excellent alternative is to present a selection of light dishes, like those suitable for the opening course of a dinner party, together with one or two main dishes.

Guests may sit at formal dining tables, in which case the buffet can include pies, roasts and other foods which are eaten with a knife and fork. If there is limited seating and the majority of guests are expected to stand during the meal, then the food must be easy to eat with a fork.

Staff may include waiters and waitresses to help guests to dishes on the buffet and a chef or competent server to carve. Make sure there are staff ready to clear dishes between courses.

Buffet Dances

A buffet for a dance may take the form of a light supper, served early on in the evening before the music starts so as not to detract from the main event, the dancing. In this case, it is wise to offer snack food very much later. On the other hand, the buffet may be more formal, as above, and this will precede

A platter of crudités is a simple, light dish for a buffet table.

the dancing but there will be equal emphasis on dining as well as dancing later. Alternatively, light snacks may be offered on trays by serving staff around the room or put out on tables for the early part of the evening and a breakfast buffet may be served in the early hours of the next day, from midnight or 12.30 a.m. onwards.

There are many variations on these ideas, with snacks being followed by a midnight feast or light refreshments of a savoury nature being made available throughout the evening.

Formal Dinner Parties

Serve good-quality bought or home-made appetizers with drinks before dinner. The meal itself may consist of four or five courses, or more. Supper dishes and one-pot dishes are usually avoided in favour of carefully sauced dishes with separate vegetables or salads. Serving a meal of many courses can be an excellent way of entertaining, particularly when guests appreciate the nuances of different foods and subtle flavours. As lighter eating has become the norm, the most acceptable way of serving such a feast is to present very small portions throughout the meal.

Caterers, butler and waiting staff may be hired for a very formal dinner party. Show the staff the facilities available beforehand, discuss the menu requirements with them in detail and provide a guest list with any notes relating to serving requirements.

The simplest of formal dinner party menus should include soup or a first course, a main course and dessert. In Europe it is also usual to serve a cheese course towards the end of the meal. A fish course or light appetizer may be served after the soup or a refreshing sorbet may be served between the first and main courses, and a savoury dish may be served instead of cheese.

Informal Dinner Parties

Three or four courses are usually served at informal dinner parties. The opening course may be a starter (appetizer), salad or soup and the main course is followed by either dessert or cheese, or both may be offered.

Informal dinner parties can feature a more extensive menu even though the general approach to the evening is very casual. For example, the confident cook may invite guests to join him or her in the kitchen before dinner as the final touches are added to the food.

If the informal nature of the evening refers more to dress than to food, then the host or hostess may still offer four or more courses but the nature of the food is likely to be less classic, with supper-style dishes (such as pasta or risotto), perhaps with a national theme, included on the menu.

Supper Parties

One or two courses may be adequate and the food can be kept very simple. The term supper indicates a casual approach to the evening in general, providing an excuse to indulge in favourite childhood dishes and an opportunity for friends to enjoy a cosy meal in the kitchen. Serving supper is an excellent way of catching up with old friends or colleagues, when everyone can feel thoroughly relaxed and allow time for conversation to drift without fear of ruining any culinary masterpieces.

Party Events

Generally, these are larger events where the food offered is less central to the proceedings, although a formal buffet served for a wedding breakfast, for instance, involves the full panoply of a well-balanced meal. For most party events, offer a good range of nibbles (snacks) and finger foods.

After-Theatre Supper

Inviting guests back for supper after a theatre performance is a good way of entertaining simply but stylishly at weekends when everyone is happy to eat late and stay into the early hours. Select a menu that can be prepared ahead: any hot food should be quick to cook with the minimum of fuss. Alternatively, simply serve a splendid array of open sandwiches, prepared in advance ready for receiving their garnish, with salad; followed by a simple dessert.

Colourful canapés for the cocktail hour.

Cocktail Parties

The food at cocktail parties is intended to whet the appetite rather than satisfy it − guests are intended to go on to a main meal elsewhere − although another school of thought decrees that cocktail snacks should be substantial to counteract the inebriating effects of the cocktails themselves. Canapés or hors d'oeuvres, nibbles (snacks) and dips are the usual refreshments. They should be served in bite-sized portions and all be easy to eat with the fingers while balancing a glass at the same time. Any messy foods should be served on cocktail sticks (toothpicks).

Mealtime Events

These are occasions when an event provides the pretext for the meal, such as a Thanksgiving or Christmas get-together, and is the focus of attention. Its style can be as formal or informal as you please, but its content needs to reflect tradition and be appropriate for the time of day.

Perfect Petits Fours

Individual servings of petits fours artfully arranged will round off any meal. Arrange the petits fours in small fluted paper or foil cases.

❖ Use a standard meringue mixture to pipe button-sized meringues and dry them out in the coolest possible oven. Sandwich them in pairs by dipping their bases in melted dark bitter chocolate.

❖ Stuff fresh dates with marzipan (almond paste) and roll in caster (superfine) sugar.

❖ Sandwich pecan nut or walnut halves in pairs with marzipan (almond paste).

Cream teas are a special treat.

Tea

Depending on numbers, afternoon tea may be simple or elaborate. When casually inviting one or two friends to tea, then sandwiches and cakes are ideal. Guests can sit in easy chairs indoors or out with plates on their knees and cups on occasional tables.

❖ For a special cream tea, offer guests scones with jam and Devonshire or clotted cream as well as sandwiches and cakes. This is an occasion for sitting around the table.

❖ A summer tea party in the garden provides an occasion to invite larger numbers – space permitting. In this case, a good selection of sandwiches and savoury foods may be offered. Cakes and biscuits, strawberries and cream or a more elaborate trifle or selection of fancy pastries may be served buffet-style.

❖ A traditional British high tea provides a great opportunity for family entertaining. This is a cross between tea and supper, and usually consists of a light egg, fish or meat course followed by teabread, buns and cakes, with tea to drink. Suitable dishes include quiche, cold meats with pickles and filled pastries.

Lunch or Luncheon

This can be an occasion for meeting friends over a light snack, for sharing activities before or after a more substantial but less elegant snack, or for bringing together a larger gathering at a buffet meal.

❖ A cold buffet is ideal for luncheon parties. Alternatively, a hot dish can be served along with a selection of salads and cold platters.

❖ Serve a vast tureen of hearty soup,

Serve light, easy-to-prepare dishes for an informal lunch gathering.

some crusty bread and cheese for an informal lunch. Minestrone is the ideal winter soup; chilled Spanish gazpacho is refreshing for summer.

❖ A traditional British Sunday lunch – a roasted joint of beef, lamb or pork, followed by a hearty dessert – may be shared with family or friends. Offer three courses, and coffee to finish. A classic roast requires fairly careful timing, so this type of meal is best kept informal.

Breakfast and Brunch

Breakfast parties are ideal for weekends and national holidays. The menu should reflect the time of day, with fruit, cereals, cold meats, breads and buns or muffins. Fruit juice, mineral water and perhaps a champagne drink to which orange juice has been added are suitable cold refreshments; coffee or tea should also be served.

Brunch is served somewhere between breakfast and lunch, usually mid-morning. It may consist of a two-

or three-course meal, or a buffet. Since guests are not expected to have eaten breakfast and the meal is not followed by lunch, brunch may well be more substantial than for a lunch menu. Alternatively, the menu may revolve around one food, such as waffles or pancakes served with a variety of sweet or savoury fillings and toppings.

Children's Parties

Apart from a special cake, the food is not usually of great gastronomic concern when planning a children's party. A mixture of savoury and sweet foods may be served as a sit-down lunch or tea, or you could opt for a buffet-style spread, depending on the age of the children and the surroundings. It is best to prepare simple, traditional foods – most children prefer them – and to limit the amount of sweet or very rich items available. Excited children will be more concerned with activities and entertainments once they have satisfied their hunger pangs.

HELPING HANDS

the ultimate in party organizing – a traditional wedding at home. Many people have nightmares at the thought of being responsible for guest lists, a menu, caterers, wine, the welfare of all the family and keeping everyone in the local community happy. The answer is to stay calm, research all the options and allow sufficient time to plan all aspects of the party. Then you can make sure you have enough of the help you need and can afford in the days leading up to the party and on the day itself.

Whether your helping hands belong to family and friends or to hired professionals, good planning is vital. Compile a list of tasks and a timetable of what to do when so that you can brief your assistants quite precisely about their duties. Once you know these aspects of the event are in capable hands, you will be able to turn your full attention to your own responsibilities as host or hostess.

Even if you are super-organized and extremely confident, you will probably appreciate help at some level when planning a party. For a small event at home you may simply seek the encouragement and moral support of a friend or partner at the planning stage and some practical assistance on the day. For a somewhat larger gathering you will almost certainly need help to make sure that the occasion runs smoothly and that you have a chance to enjoy it yourself. This is particularly true for large formal events, especially for

FRIENDS AND RELATIVES

When planning informal parties or small, formal gatherings, it is probably enough to draw on those about you for any help you need rather than hiring professional assistance. If you do ask friends or relatives for special help, or accept assistance when it is volunteered, it is vital to establish a clear and tactful understanding to avoid any time-wasting, confusion and offence later. Before allowing anyone to help, consult your lists of work to be completed, decide exactly what you want to do, and can realistically tackle, yourself, then look at the areas with which you need help. Never fall into the trap of gratefully accepting every offer of help without organizing the distribution of work, otherwise you may find that the party has started early while you run around trying to get all the vital finishing touches completed.

❖ Always enlist the support of the family or other household members. Even if they are not involved in the organization of the party they must at least be supportive and not cause any hindrance. This point applies particularly to children, younger teenagers and partners who are unused to helping with household tasks, as they can get in the way dreadfully!

❖ All adults in the household should play their part, if not with direct preparation for the party, then at least with making sure that the home is neat and tidy.

❖ Delegate responsibility for specific tasks only to those who are competent and enthusiastic. Do not force someone into something he or she obviously does not want to do, as you will end up having to pick up the pieces right at the last minute.

❖ Never feel obliged or forced to accept help from someone whom you do not want involved. Some people will eagerly, and often unthinkingly, try to take over the whole show, or take over a major part which you would prefer to play. It is best to divert their attention tactically to an area which you are prepared to delegate. Alternatively, firmly but pleasantly thank them for their offer and point out that the work is already in hand.

❖ When you do enlist the help of others, clearly plan their roles with them, making sure they understand what needs doing and how you want it done. This may seem to be a very pedantic way of handling volunteers, but it is practical.

❖ Remember to encourage and thank everyone who helps, no matter how small the contribution. Never dismiss or overlook good intentions.

❖ For occasions such as formal engagement parties and weddings, it is diplomatic to involve members of the partner's family or close friends. Never exclude them from plans. Welcome their input into the proceedings and offer assistance, and deal tactfully with any suggestions which may not fit in with the general flow of plans.

PROFESSIONAL HELP

You may decide to employ a company to organize the party completely, leaving you free to concentrate on the guest list and the social side of the occasion. You will probably find several local companies offering comprehensive party services, from organizing a children's birthday party to formal dinner dances and weddings with live music or a disc jockey.

When paying for any help, it is a good idea to ask around among friends for recommendations. If you were impressed by outside staff at a gathering you attended and know the organizers well enough, then don't hesitate to ask for their comments.

Cleaning Services

If you have a regular home help, then warn him or her of your party plans and book time for special preparations, and for clearing up afterwards. Some helpers will also assist immediately at the end of the party with washing up and clearing away.

If you do not have a regular cleaner, then you may consider using an agency or a company which moves in and spring cleans the house on an appointed day. Book a window cleaner shortly before the date of the event. For daytime parties and in summer particularly it is a good idea to have all the windows sparkling clean.

Comprehensive Party Planning

Draw up a list of your requirements, then approach suitable companies in your area for their comments and a quotation. Look through their suggestions carefully and go back to those companies offering the most attractive and competitive packages with more specific queries. Ask about previous events which they have organized,

how long they have been operating and how far in advance you have to supply a firm booking. When planning a large wedding or similar function, many hosts or hostesses think in terms of contacting suitable companies up to a year ahead, especially for spring and summer weddings, when popular organizers quickly fill their diaries.

Caterers

You can commission caterers to provide all or some of the food, to provide food and waiting staff, or to organize all aspects of the meal, including tables, seating, linen, crockery (china), cutlery (flatware), the menu, wine, chef or cook and waiting staff. Whether you opt for a large company or an individual cook depends mainly on the number of guests. There are many small caterering outfits which work from home, and which offer excellent quality buffets and service at gatherings for anything up to a hundred

people. Individual cooks can also perform well for dinner parties, and will sometimes wait at table.

It's best to approach a number of caterers initially, give them some idea of the function and numbers involved, and ask them what type of food and service they provide and what menus they would recommend, before getting quotes from a shortlist.

Discuss numbers, facilities for catering and serving food, the exact style of food and meal required and some indication of budget before receiving a menu suggestion. By making sure the caterer has all the necessary information you will avoid wasting time on discussing unsuitable menus. If you have queries or are unhappy about any aspect of the menu, then follow up promptly and come to a decision. Larger companies will provide a written order; if you verbally make any changes, then follow by writing a letter outlining them.

If necessary, enlist a skillful hand with flower arrangements.

You may want to hand over responsibility for the wine to the caterers; some may work on the premiss that they always expect to handle wine orders when organizing functions. However, the more economical option is to deal with this yourself, particularly as many good wine merchants will advise on fine wines; there is even more choice in the middle-market area.

If the cook or caterers provide waiting staff, china and so on, then you can expect them to organize staff and return the goods.

Waiting Staff

You may decide to employ a waiter or waitress for formal dinners which you prepare yourself, in which case it is important to find someone who is confident and capable enough to interact correctly with yourself while you cook and look after your guests. With careful planning, this arrangement can work very well and ease the burden on you. Pay attention to serving arrangements when planning the menu, selecting dishes which can easily be brought to table and served. The waiter or waitress should clear the table after the first course. Make sure the waiter or waitress is organized as far as the side dishes are concerned, then ask him or her to bring them in promptly once you have presented the main course. You or your partner may serve or carve the main course, leaving your helper to place vegetable dishes on the table. The waiter or waitress should clear the table and, depending on the dish, bring in dessert, then coffee.

If you wish food to be served to guests, make sure that the waiter or waitress is experienced in doing so correctly, presenting dishes to the diner's left.

At drinks or cocktail parties, trays of canapés and snacks can be handed around by a server, who will also remove used glasses and top up drinks. At a buffet, he or she may assist in serving certain dishes, top up drinks and remove used items.

Ask waiting staff to arrive 30–60 minutes before guests are due, to fit in with your own schedule and requirements. Explain the menu and facilities, and make a note to pass on any relevant information about guests that they may need to know. Offer a cup of tea or a soft drink if time allows.

Hiring a Butler

Most special occasions that call for hired help will not, of course, include the services of a butler. However, some caterers do offer a butler service, and it's useful to know exactly what this entails. On the other hand, you may want to instruct one of the waiting staff to take on some of the functions of a traditional butler.

❖ The duties of the butler are to prepare the table for a dinner, to set out glasses and ensure that all drinks and wines are ready. If there are waiters, waitresses or bar staff, then the butler should oversee their work to ensure that all runs smoothly. The butler opens the door, takes coats and announces guests. During a sit-down meal the butler may carve or do all the serving if there are no waiting staff. He will also serve coffee and liqueurs.

❖ At buffets and any other large parties, the butler will top up drinks and generally ensure that all guests are well cared for; however, although he may hand out some canapés or hors d'oeuvre and remove used dishes, the butler is not expected to serve food at buffets.

❖ Make sure the butler is shown around before the party, that he arrives in time to lay a dinner table (and is aware of this duty in advance) and that he knows where to put guests' coats. Go through details of the area to which guests should be shown and how you would like guests introduced.

Magicians and jugglers can liven up a party where children are present.

Bartender Employing someone to look after the bar is only necessary if the function demands that cocktails are mixed. Waiters, waitresses and butler all serve drinks.

ENTERTAINMENT

The form of entertainment depends on the guests and the occasion. The majority of dinner or drinks parties run perfectly smoothly without any formal entertainment; sometimes music and dancing are an essential feature of a gathering; and children's parties often rely on well-organized entertainment.

If you plan games, make sure all the equipment you need is ready to hand and assign someone who knows the rules to take charge of the proceedings. If you want music, whether it is for

background interest or for dancing, it is a good idea to delegate the task of organizing it to someone enthusiastic and knowledgeable. They might prepare tapes beforehand, or act as a disc jockey, adapting the music to the mood of the party.

If you want guests to dance, then it is vital to make sure that there is a sufficiently large area cleared for the purpose. The host and/or hostess starts the dancing by inviting other guests to participate in the fun.

Musicians

Live bands, pianists, string quartets and various musical groups may all be hired. Discuss the repertoire when booking and confirm details a week or so before the party. Live music is well suited to events such as weddings or large parties when a hall is hired or a marquee or tent erected. Unless you have a very large area in your home, then anything more than a pianist may be very overpowering as a form of general entertainment.

Entertainers

Magicians and clowns can be booked for children's parties, and for adult parties where children are included. Their performance will revive any flagging spirits, particularly those of children who are bored among too many adults. If you intend to entertain all age groups, discuss this with prospective entertainers and make sure they have a suitable repertoire.

Entertainers of this sort are often used to working at functions where guests are seated, not necessarily in rows but at least at dining tables. They may not adapt easily to moving among guests who are standing. For parties where children and adults are invited or at weddings where there are lots of children, it can be an excellent idea to organize all the youngsters into sitting in the living room or a suitable place for the entertainment. Since they all sit quite happily on the floor this does not usually involve a great deal of work and a 20-minute show can provide a quiet gap which will be appreciated by adults as well as giving younger children a rest from running around.

Outdoor Amusements for Children

Puppet shows provide the outdoor equivalent of the conjuring show, with a performance at a pre-set time that makes a rewarding focus for everyone's attention. Even though puppet shows are intended for children, many adults will happily break away from socializing to participate. An alternative form of entertainment to offer out of doors is "activity equipment" such as play centres. These are designed for children's parties, but most adults love to try them out, too.

When hiring any equipment of this kind, make sure you have a clear understanding about what the fee covers. Some companies sound extremely economical but leave the collection and process of erecting equipment to you.

OUTSIDE ENTERTAINMENT

Local telephone directories list a variety of different entertainment possibilities, as do local newspapers and some up-market glossy magazines. Personal recommendations from friends are always helpful, particularly if you are thinking of employing musicians or other live entertainment such as a disco for an adults' party.

Discos

Even though discos are sometimes thought of as noisy teenage entertainment, there are outfits that specialize in providing suitable music for weddings and family gatherings. Again, it is important to discuss the repertoire to suit all guests. Consider noise levels and ensure you do not cause offence to neighbours.

STUNNING SETTINGS

*T*he first sight of the table plays a keynote for any meal, so it is essential that the setting is just right for the occasion. In contemporary living-dining rooms and at buffet parties the table is on display from the moment the guests arrive; if guests happen to pass an open dining room door as they pass through the hallway before dinner, the merest glimpse of arrangements should excite the dining instincts by hinting at the quality of the meal to come.

Whether crisp and sophisticated, softly flowing with lace and flowers, warm and homely, or refreshingly bright, the setting should confirm the guests' anticipation of the party and raise it to new levels. This section is designed to arouse your enthusiasm for scene-setting and to encourage artistic instincts. With flair and a sense of occasion you can be as individualistic as you wish, and carry off any event with outstanding success.

TABLE LINEN

There is an enormous variety of table linen available, most of it far removed from traditional white linen. There are no rules about what is acceptable or otherwise, the only qualification being that the choice should suit the occasion. A chequered patio cloth and bright paper napkins are not worthy of a gourmet meal of classic dishes. Conversely white damask and fine glass would seem inappropriate for a casual invitation for a snack lunch . . . .

White linen

White linen is both versatile and practical, and there is nothing quite like crisply starched, large white napkins for a dinner party table.

Heavy, white damask tablecloths and napkins are expensive but they will last for years. It is always worth looking out for good-quality second-hand linen at auctions, flea markets and in antique or junk shops – as long as the fabric is not scorched, badly marked, worn or torn, then it is a good buy.

Although spray starch is adequate for a tablecloth, the only way to get a really good finish on napkins is by starching them with traditional starch which you mix with boiling water. A good compromise, instead of soaking the fabric in the starch solution, is to mix a small quantity according to the packet directions, then keep it in a clean plant spray bottle. Spray dry napkins and cloths before ironing, leaving the moisture to soak into the fabric for about 30 seconds. The result is just like proper starched linen.

Although plain white linen is unsuitable for casual table settings, do not feel that it always has to form the base for extremely formal table arrangements. Introduce a contemporary air with your choice of flowers or table

White, damask table linen adds elegance to a formal dinner.

Choose brightly coloured table linen for an ethnic meal or theme party.

centrepieces; instead of traditional white candles go for coloured ones or even scented candles; or neatly roll the napkins and use colourful napkin ties or ribbons with a small flower or suitable trimming to pick up on the rest of the table decorations.

Plain and Printed Linen

Good linen in delicate pastel shades can be equally as formal as traditional white table settings. Deep colours can be more dramatic and stylish but just as formal, depending on the overall presentation. Strong colours can also make an eye-catching base for flamboyant themes, particularly when preparing an ethnic meal or for fancy dress

Table Protection

Buy a waterproof protective covering to lay on the table under the cloth. This protects the table surface from plates and glassware, and from any spills. Do not buy a cheap brand if you have a good table; it is better to spend more and know that the table is safe.

(costume) parties and buffets.

Printed and woven linen varies enormously in quality. Smart checks and stripes are useful for informal picnics, barbecues, patio meals, breakfasts and brunches.

Embroidered Linen and Lace

Colourful hand embroidery is ideal for breakfast cloths, and for table coverings for brunches, family teas and high tea. Fine work trimmed with lace and lace cloths are ideal for afternoon teas, parties in the garden, grand picnic parties and for weddings.

Appliqué Napkin

Appliqué in the form of flowers or fruit makes decorative corner trimmings for plain tablecloths and napkins.

YOU WILL NEED: plain coloured napkins, thin card (posterboard) for template, pencil, colourfast red fabric, green felt, scissors, iron-on interfacing, dressmaker's marking pen, red and yellow thread, needle.

1 Transfer the strawberry shape to the red fabric and the stem shape to the green felt. You will also need to transfer the strawberry shape onto a piece of iron-on interfacing.

2 Cut around the lines using a pair of sharp scissors. Iron on the interfacing to the back of the strawberry cut-out. Mark where the seed details will go with a dressmaker's marking pen (this should be washable).

3 Tack (baste) the strawberry cut-out in place on the napkin, then stitch all around the edge using buttonhole stitch or zig-zag machine stitch. This will prevent the fabric from fraying. Tack the stem in position, then hand or machine stitch in place using a straight stitch and yellow thread. Hand stitch the seed details using the yellow thread.

Stencilled Table Linen

Wall stencils used as part of the dining room or kitchen decor can be picked up on cloths and napkins using fabric paints. Do not try to match colours, as it is unlikely you will be able to achieve the same shade with fabric paints. Select toning or contrasting colours instead. Follow the manufacturer's instructions for using fabric paint for a result which is lasting and washable.

YOU WILL NEED: plain coloured place mats and napkins; (for making stencil) paper, pencil, sticky (transparent) tape; clear acetate for stencil, waterproof black felt-tip pen, craft knife, fabric paints, paintbrush, rag.

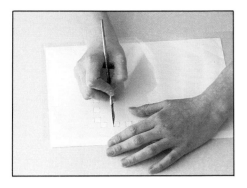

1 If you are making your own stencil, draw your design onto a sheet of paper. Place the sheet of acetate on top and tape in position to hold the sheet firmly in place. Transfer the design to the acetate using a waterproof black felt-tip pen. Cut around the outline of the stencil design with a craft knife.

2 Load the brush with paint. Keep a rag handy for wiping excess paint from the brush. For stencilling, you should not have too much paint on the brush as this can seep beneath the stencil. Holding the stencil firmly in place, press the brush over the pattern in the stencil keeping the brush vertical. Wait for the paint to dry before applying the second colour.

3 To create a stippled effect, you will need some white or pale coloured paint and a clean brush. Lightly load the brush with paint and dab on the paint using a stabbing motion. Allow the paint to dry, then fix according to the manufacturer's instructions.

A range of fine cutlery (flatware).

Collect a range of colourful china for informal entertaining.

EATING UTENSILS

It is usual to have a set of everyday cutlery (flatware) for kitchen use and to have a smart collection for dining room use. Silver or silver plate is the traditional material for eating utensils, but stainless steel is more popular and practical, and there are many elegant designs – both traditional and modern – in high-quality finishes.

For entertaining purposes, most cutlery (flatware) sets include meat knives and small knives for bread and butter; large forks and two sets of small forks, for first courses and desserts; soup spoons, dessertspoons and teaspoons; and possibly fish knives and forks, which are a useful addition. Serving spoons are essential; sauce and soup ladles can be useful.

Remember that cutlery (flatware) with wood or bone handles must not be immersed in water for any length of time, so they are not suitable for dishwashers. Make sure the handles are clear of the water if soaked.

Simple designs are often the most elegant.

CHINAWARE

Traditionally, there is usually a set or mixture of crockery (china) in everyday use and a set reserved for smarter meals. China for special occasions consists of dinner and salad plates, soup bowls, dessert plates and bowls, and tea or coffee cups and saucers, usually of the best quality affordable.

❖ White china is practical and versatile as it may be dressed up or down by the table settings. It also allows plenty of scope for buying ovenproof dishes and serving dishes which do not clash with the dinner service.

❖ Build up a collection of bright everyday china, including soup bowls which double as pasta dishes, so that it can be used for informal entertaining.

❖ Good-quality old china can be attractive. Given that you collect china of a similar or complementary style, the patterns do not have to match. For example, large floral patterns on serving bowls, cake stands and dishes make a pleasing display on a buffet table.

❖ If you have a dishwasher, check when buying new fine china that any decorative finish will not be affected by the machine.

Unusual Serving Containers

The most unlikely of serving dishes can often look wonderful, especially at large parties when your usual supply is stretched to the limit. Search in junk shops and antique shops for old, decorative china (check before you buy for cracks and chips) and use casseroles and vegetable dishes for pâtés.

❖ Large wash jugs and basins which are in good condition make attractive, exciting serving vessels: use the jug for outrageously fruity punches and fill the bowl with a dessert such as fruit salad.

❖ Dress up inferior glass cake stands with luxurious bows of ribbon and use the very readily available glass sugar bowls for serving salad dressing.

❖ If all else fails and you really cannot find suitable serving dishes, then buy some large white plastic trays and decorate them according to the food on offer or the party: cover them with paper doilies; tie ribbon bows and stick them on the corners; wire frosted flowers or fruit and tape them to the corners; or use festive decorations such as sprigs of holly or spring flowers.

GLASSWARE

Choice of glassware is entirely personal and subject to budget. When buying inexpensive glasses, remember that it is always pleasing to be offered a glass that is suitable for the contents and comfortable to hold. Plain styles are generally preferable to ornate ones. Always hold each type (even if they are a special offer at the local hardware store) as you would if you were about to drink. Look at the way in which the stems join to the bowls – are they smoothly incorporated or is there an ugly link? – and always run your fingers around the rim to check there are no rough edges.

If you regularly have barbecues and parties which demand inexpensive, functional glasses, then it is worth buying a boxful of white wine goblets and storing them for such occasions.

Good-quality glass is always pleasing when drinking wine, but this does not mean having very expensive or decorative crystal; the simplest, fine-rim glasses, which are often the most inexpensive, are often the nicest from which to drink, especially when serving light white wine, which tends to be lost in heavily cut lead crystal.

The number of glasses provided at a dinner party depends on the wines served. Always provide water glasses and separate glasses for white and red wine. You also need glasses for serving pre-dinner drinks and for brandy, port or liqueurs after dinner.

Sturdy plastic tumblers are essential for children's parties and for any occasions when lots of children are invited. Although decorative plastic patio wear looks the part, it is not pleasing material from which to drink wine. A better option for outdoor parties and picnics would be inexpensive plain glasses – wrap them up well in tea-towels (dish-towels) when transporting them or keep them in the boxes in which they were purchased.

Shapes and Sizes of Glass

Liqueur glasses are the smallest, followed by port, then sherry glasses. White wine glasses are smaller than those for red wine. Hock glasses originally designed for German white wine have tall stems and rounded bowls. Champagne and sparkling wines are served in flutes, tall slim glasses which conserve the gas in the wine. The once popular wide-topped champagne glasses did nothing for the wine, and they could also be very poorly balanced when filled! Water goblets are larger than red wine glasses.

There is a wide range of glassware for pre-dinner and after-dinner drinks, parties and cocktails. It is just as important to choose well in this area as it is when buying wine glasses. There are a few traditional shapes and associations.

❖ A jigger is a small glass which holds 45 ml/1½ fl oz and this is the standard measure used when mixing cocktails. It is ideal for serving very strong drinks, such as Polish vodka.

❖ Cocktail glasses are traditionally about 75 ml/3 fl oz (about ⅓ cup) capacity with steeply sloping sides. Sizes vary and there are some large cocktail glasses which can be lethal when filled with strong drinks!

❖ An 'old-fashioned' glass is a short, wide, heavy-bottomed tumbler, about 250 ml/8 fl oz (1 cup) capacity; this is ideal for the cocktail of the same name, consisting of whiskey (rye or bourbon) a little sugar syrup, Angostura bitters, ice, a cherry and lemon.

❖ A highball glass is a tall, slim, heavy-bottomed glass tumbler, about 250 ml/8 fl oz (1 cup) capacity.

❖ Beer and cider (hard cider) may be served in tall tumblers or stemmed glasses. The classic glass for light beers has a short wide stem and tall slim bowl (a lager glass). Goblets with short stems and large, often well-rounded, bowls are also used for beers. Very large, well-rounded glasses on tall stems (often intended for those who imbibe red wine with pleasure) are excellent for serving beers and ciders. Metal tankards and mugs are less elegant but there are many attractive glasses of this type.

❖ Punch may be served in a punch bowl with matching cups. Round-bowled glasses are also suitable or use short, fairly small water glasses.

❖ Brandy glasses have large bowls, narrowing at the rim, and short stems. They are designed for swirling and sniffing, to appreciate the aroma of the drink as well as its flavour.

❖ Irish coffee glasses are slim and tall, with short, wide stems and a handle. They are also useful for serving mulled wine as they are easy to hold even when the contents are very warm.

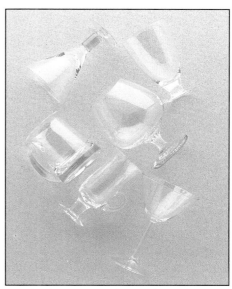

Drinks glasses vary in shape and size.

Choose glassware that is suitable for the contents and pleasing to hold.

Brightly coloured china is extremely versatile. Dress it up or down according to the occasion.

TABLE SETTINGS

The way in which the table is set depends on the occasion and the type of food being served. The convention is to place forks to the left of the plate and knives and spoons to the right.

The forks are laid with tines pointing up and the spoons have bowls up. The base of each is about 2.5 cm/1 in from the table edge. Spoons and forks for dessert are sometimes laid across the top of the plate, along with the knife

for cheese. A bread plate is placed on the left side and the napkin is usually laid across it. The napkin may also be folded decoratively and placed in the middle of the setting. Napkins are not placed in glasses for formal settings.

Formal Settings

When you want to pull out all the stops and serve a number of courses laying a traditional table is simple.

❖ The rule is that the diner starts at the outside of the row of cutlery (flatware) and works inwards. Working inwards from the right: bread knife, soup spoon, fish knife or knife for first course, meat knife, dessertspoon. Working inwards from the left: fish fork or fork for

first course, fork for main course, fork for dessert. This is the most formal method of laying place settings, the cutlery being suited to each course in turn. Knives and forks for fruit or a savoury offering at the end of the meal may be brought in when the course is served. If the dessert is eaten with a spoon only, it is usual to lay this on the table for formal settings.

❖ The spoon and fork for dessert may be laid across the top of the

plate, spoon with handle to the right, fork handle to the left. This is still acceptable as a formal setting, but not quite up to traditional state dinner standards!

❖ The glasses are set out above the cutlery to the right of the place setting. They should be arranged in the order in which they are used, but the conventions relating to placing glass are not as rigid as for cutlery – make sure, however, that all glass settings are identical.

FINGER BOWLS These are provided, one to each guest, when the food has to be eaten with the fingers. For example, when peeling prawns (shrimp), cracking and cleaning lobster, eating globe artichokes and serving whole fruit at the end of the meal. The bowls should be fairly small and wide-topped; glass is ideal. The bowls are placed on small plates, saucers or delicate cotton mats. The water should be warm and a slice of lemon, rose petals or other suitable decorative ingredient may be added.

SERVING SPOONS Serving spoons and forks may be laid at intervals on the table and there may be heatproof mats ready for hot dishes. At formal meals where food is served to the diners by waiting staff this is unnecessary. When serving utensils are laid, these should follow the convention of having spoon handles to the right and fork handles to the left. Any special serving implements for the host or hostess should be laid near his or her place or brought in with the food.

CRUETS AND CONDIMENTS

Traditionally, salt and pepper sets are placed on the table and several are laid for large gatherings. If the cook has carefully prepared and tasted the food for seasoning, however, then he or she may not provide salt.

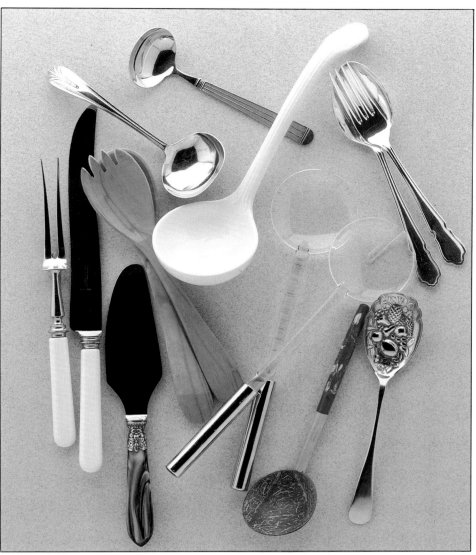

Above: a range of serving utensils.

Below: a finger bowl with rose petals.

Pepper can be another matter as there are times when freshly ground pepper enhances an ingredient, for example fresh figs, some melons, Parma ham (prosciutto), pasta dishes and goats' cheese are typical. A pepper mill for table use should be presentable and it is best to buy one especially for the purpose. Avoid buying an attractive case with a poor-quality grinding mechanism: look for a smart but workmanlike utensil instead. Mills are usually filled with black pepper.

Condiments such as mustard are laid to one side, and several containers should be placed on a large table.

A garland of fresh flowers and foliage enhances an outdoor buffet table.

BUFFET SETTINGS

Buffet tables provide the perfect excuse for impressive settings, perhaps with swags of flowers or ribbons and posies as well as a large main decoration. All the food should be decorative too, and it must be arranged for ease of access when guests serve themselves.

The buffet may be placed against a wall so that guests move along in front of the table and serve themselves, or it may be situated in the middle of a room (or with space all around) so that guests move around the table. Whichever system is used, there should be an obvious starting point for serving and this is indicated by a pile of plates. On a large table, plates may be piled at both ends so that guests can work from both directions.

If the buffet is set against a wall, then the main decoration should be at the

Small garlands look pretty above entrances.

rear and positioned in the centre. If guests walk all around the table, then a centrepiece should be placed on the table.

Make sure all the dishes are easy to reach and that there are serving spoons nearby. If there is a ham or other food which needs carving, set it in a position to one side of the table so that guests do not obstruct access to other dishes while they carve. It should be someone's task to check the availability of foods, topping dishes up and tidying the buffet occasionally.

Set napkins and cutlery separately on a side table. Large paper napkins are usually used for informal buffets. If disposable plates are used, they should be sturdy and of good quality, as thin plates sag miserably and make eating difficult. Buffet-style plates are now available which include a holder for a wine glass. Alternatively, keep a large number of good-quality, large plastic plates, which are ideal for entertaining in large numbers. They are easier to rinse, stack and wash than china plates, and ideal for outdoor parties as well as for informal buffets.

Themed Settings

There are times when it is fun to abandon convention and go for something strikingly different in the way of setting arrangements. This is fine if you know the guests reasonably well, but it is not a good idea to confront business acquaintances or people you rarely meet with something out of the ordinary. Think of these setting styles as informal alternatives!

White and pastels tend to be favoured colours for table settings, but strong colours make a dramatic impact. A blue and gold setting, for example, could have a deep blue cloth and napkins, matching candles and a blue flower arrangement, such as hydrangeas, hyacinths, delphiniums, lavender or cornflowers. Wire dried autumn leaves and spray them gold, then use these with the fresh flowers.

Alternatively, try creating a lush green table using a white linen cloth as the base and limiting the other colour to green, including candles. Make a central arrangement of leaves: as well as cuttings from shrubs, take leaves from indoor plants, such as Japanese aralia and grape ivy. Create movement and interest by using leaves of different sizes and shapes.

A contrast setting could start with a black tablecloth and white dinner plates. Use black-and-white napkins, perhaps ones that have a strong, geometric pattern. To make an elongated napkin shape with points at the top and bottom, fold and press each

Combine clean lines and black and white chinaware and table linen for a strikingly modern look.

napkin into quarters, then give it a quarter turn and fold the opposite side corners over the middle so that they overlap. Press neatly and place one on each plate.

Use small white candle holders and short black candles, or small white saucers and black nightlights (votive-style candles) or small, rounded candles. Place several of these along the length of a rectangular table or around the middle of a circular table. If using white saucers, press and fold two small squares of crêpe paper to sit under the candles: one black square to go on the saucer, then a white square offset on top to go under the candle.

Any central decoration should be simple and based on white flowers with dried leaves that are wired and sprayed black.

In complete contrast, a pretty lace setting is ideal for a celebratory lunch party, for a small wedding lunch party or for a large buffet table. Lay a plain-coloured cloth or fabric over the table – pink is ideal for this theme. The colour should be reasonably strong but not garish. Lay a lace cloth over the plain cloth so that the colour shows through.

Opposite: fine lace and small posies of flowers set the scene for a celebration lunch.

Candles and candle holders come in a wide range of sizes and colours suitable for every occasion.

Lighting for Effect

Fixing on the right lighting is crucial to the success of any scene-setting plan and the results can have marked effects on your guests. Just as people will feel uncomfortable in glaringly bright surroundings more conducive to a dentist's office than to a dinner party, so they will also feel unnerved and depressed by lighting which is dim to the point of being gloomy.

For the majority of entertaining the lighting should be soft enough to make your guests look their best and to suggest that everyone ought to be relaxed. It should, however, be bright enough for people to see what is being eaten and to read the expressions across the dining table.

Candles

Candles really do give a room a pleasing glow. They should be used in conjunction with sufficient electric light to ensure that the surroundings are bright enough.
❖ Slim, tall candles are perfect for elegant dining.
❖ Chubby, bright candles are well suited to kitchen suppers and informal meals.

❖ Create different heights of light by arranging candles around the room. Place some on a fireplace hearth (set them to one side if the fire is lit, otherwise they melt and run), others on side tables and some at windowsill level.
❖ Arrange marbles or glass pebbles in a large copper or other metal bowl with nightlights. Place the bowl on a low table or footstool in a corner of the room.

❖ Wherever you place candles, make absolutely sure that they present no risk of fire and never leave lit candles unattended.
❖ Floating candles are designed for floating when alight. Select a wide-topped glass bowl and place some colourful stones, shells and artificial aquarium plants in the bowl. Float and light the candles.
❖ Combine floating candles and Japanese water flowers.

Floating candles and rosebuds in a bowl.

Set conventional place settings. Roll the napkins and tie them with satin ribbon and large bows.

Draw up the lace cloth at the corners of the table and at intervals around the edge (between place settings), then pin it in place so that it hangs in swags.

Prepare small posies of roses and tie them with flamboyant bows of satin ribbon to match the place settings. Pin the flowers on the cloth.

Arrange a large bowl of roses for the centre of the table. Make sure you have enough roses to lay one at each place

setting. Trim each stem and wrap with a leaf in a little moistened absorbent kitchen paper (paper towels). A final wrapping of foil will hold everything together and keep in the moisture. Place the roses under the bows around the napkins shortly before guests arrive.

Candles

White candles are traditional at formal dinners but this convention depends entirely on the hostess and the setting. Tall candlesticks usually have short candles and short holders take long candles. The candles may be placed in the centre of the table or at intervals along its length. If there is the space, very effective settings can be created by flouting this convention and arranging low candles or nightlights (votive-style candles) towards the table corners.

Ideas for Electric Lights

❖ Arrange fans or sunshades in front of floor spotlights to create a warm light.
❖ Make large paper lanterns and place very low-wattage bulbs in them (15 watt).
❖ Use coloured bulbs. These are especially good for lively parties,

where areas may be lit with bright red, blue or green by fitting the appropriate bulbs.
❖ Use a floor spotlight or standard spotlight to cast light from behind a large, exotic-looking indoor plant – the effect can be quite eerie.
❖ Place a low-wattage light on a windowsill to illuminate a hand-painted blind or unusual fabric.

Patio and Garden Settings

If you are entertaining outdoors, the patio must be swept clean and adorned with flowers. Tubs of growing plants and hanging baskets should be distributed. Table settings may be bright or pastel, as you prefer and according to the occasion: pastels are ideal for special celebrations; primary colours for fun events.

Entertaining outdoors can be just another day in the garden or the whole scene can be transformed by bringing out a few props and distributing them in a casual fashion. The key to success with this sort of scene-setting is to really go for it . . . do not feel shy about being flamboyant: anything less will not command the same stunning impact. Take a careful look at the arrangement of garden chairs and patio furniture. Bring out rugs and large comfortable cushions. As well as a sunshade for the table, put up smaller sunshades and leave them lying around

Transform a simple straw hat with a garland of fresh or dried flowers.

for guests to use – Oriental sunshades are inexpensive and decorative. Buy simple straw hats, decorate them with ribbons and flowers and scatter them around both as decoration and for guests' use. Decorate shrubs and trees with enormous bows of ribbon and balloons. Hang round flower or foliage posies around the outside of the house and from large standard sunshades.

If the party is planned for late afternoon or evening, then light garden flares (torches) and set lights among shrubs or trees – do not create a fire hazard, however. Outdoor candles can be purchased in special glass holders which withstand the heat and prevent the flame from blowing out in a breeze. Coloured glass holders create attractive shadows and colours.

Candles in glass holders cast a warm glow on the patio once the sun has gone down. Be careful to place them in a safe position.

Gold Leaf Napkin Ring

Collect autumn leaves to make this elegant napkin ring. Dried beech leaves have been used here, but any medium-sized dried leaves are suitable. As an alternative, use silver spray to paint.

YOU WILL NEED: dried leaves, wire, gold spray paint, florists' dry foam (styro foam), heavy satin ribbon, needle and matching thread.

1 For each napkin ring, wire 3 dried leaves onto 20 cm/8 in wires.

2 Spray the wired leaves with gold spray paint on a well-protected work surface. Always work in a well-ventilated area. Stand each finished leaf in florists' dry foam (styro foam) to dry.

3 When the paint is dry, twist the leaves together. Arrange the leaves so that the central leaf is higher than the other two leaves. Allow about 2.5 cm/1 in of wire to remain untwisted immediately below the leaves when they have been arranged.

4 Wrap the end of the ribbon around the wire below the middle leaf, taking about 7.5 cm/3 in of the end and binding it around the twisted wire. Bind another layer of ribbon over this, then bind along the length of the wire.

5 Stitch the ribbon in place at the end of the wire with matching thread. Trim off any protuding ends of wire. Form the ribboned wire into a ring and secure the end under the leaves with a few stitches. Gently twist the leaves in place and flatten the ring to neaten.

Greenery Chain

Make a simple chain of greenery to swag the table edge.

YOU WILL NEED: suitable foliage, plastic-covered tying wire or florists' wire, selection of herbs such as bay leaves, rosemary and thyme, needle and green thread, pins, green ribbon.

1 Join lengths of foliage together with suitable wire cut into manageable strips.

2 Wire sprigs of herbs and stitch them to the chain at intervals. Pin the chain to one corner of the table and then pin at each sprig of herbs to form swags. Trim with bows of green ribbon.

Pomander Decorations

Orange and lemon pomanders are pretty hung around the kitchen suspended from ribbon, or arranged in a bowl as a table centrepiece. Stud them all over with cloves to keep longer.

YOU WILL NEED: oranges and lemons, soft pencil, cloves, ribbon, pins.

1 Using a soft pencil, lightly mark segments lengthways on the fruit. Press the cloves along the pencilled lines, spacing them evenly.

2 Take a length of ribbon and wrap it lengthways on the fruit, positioning it between two rows of cloves. Tie it off at one end. Repeat, tying off the second ribbon in the same position as the first.

3 Take a separate piece of ribbon and thread it under the knot of the ribbon on the fruit. Tie it into a bow and insert a pin through the ribbon and into the fruit to hold it in place. The pin may be disguised by folding one loose end of the ribbon over the join and tucking it under.

Garden Posy

Spherical posies of fresh, dried or bright tissue flowers on a length of garden cane (bamboo stake) and placed in flower pots can be arranged around the patio and garden to provide instant colour.

YOU WILL NEED: sturdy florists' dry foam (styro foam) spheres, garden cane, ribbon, flower pot, sand, gravel, moss, flowers and foliage.

1 Place the foam sphere on the end of a cut piece of garden cane (bamboo stake) which has first been wound around with ribbon. Insert the cane into a flower pot filled with sand or gravel, then cover the top of the pot with moss. Begin to insert the flowers into the foam.

2 Add foliage to fill any gaps.

3 Finish by attaching a ribbon bow into the foam at the base of the arrangement.

DRINKS FOR ALL TASTES

The days of high-jinks and free-flowing cocktails have been replaced by comparatively sober gatherings; however, despite this practical approach, the whole business of liquid refreshment still adds a zing to many occasions. This is now balanced by a welcome safe attitude to alcohol, which means that there must always be appropriate soft drinks such as fruit juices and mineral water for those who are driving or, indeed, travelling by any means.

The following pages set out to boost the confidence of those who are unsure about what type of drink to serve and to encourage a cosmopolitan, adventurous attitude to wine. It is quite in order, these days, to nurture an individual approach to apertifs and drinks served with a meal but there are ways of doing this well, with a few reasons for observing some conventions on wine and food. Treat conventions as a framework for your own ideas, without allowing them to quell your likes and dislikes, and you will surely carry off the most formal occasions, with the most experienced of imbibers, with admirable style.

APERITIFS

An aperitif is a drink served before a meal, either luncheon or dinner, for the purpose of exciting the taste buds and arousing the appetite. For this reason, drinks served before food should, in theory, be dry and simple, almost with a zesty tang. Individual taste obviously tames this opinion and there are those who will always select a sweet drink regardless of the occasion. Drinks such as sherry, vermouth and some spirits are typical traditional aperitifs; wines are served more frequently these days and light beers should be available for anyone who wants to quench a thirst. White port and dry Madeira (Sercial) both make good aperitifs.

Sherry

This fortified wine ranges from very dry to sweet. Fino sherries are dry, aromatic and pale; manzanilla is a very dry, fino sherry with a delicate taste and pale colour. Amontillado is medium dry, with a fuller flavour than the finos from which it is made. Oloroso is a very sweet sherry with a full flavour and rich, dark colour.

Cream sherry is also very sweet and traditionally dark and rich. Pale cream sherries are also sweet but they are not as rich as the dark cream wine. It is important to buy good-quality sherry for drinking.

Sherry is traditionally served at room temperature in a small glass or double-sized sherry schooner. The alternative method is to serve the wine, usually a dry or very dry type of sherry, on ice. Guests should always be given the option. A white wine glass or attractive stemmed aperitif glass should be used when sherry is served on ice.

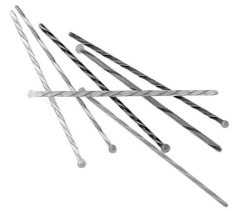

Vermouth

Vermouth is a wine-based aperitif, usually flavoured with herbs. There are red and white types, the red being very rich and sweet, and the white available as very dry, dry or sweet. The quality of the drink varies according to the brand, although with less pronounced differences than for sherry.

Vermouth may be served on ice, usually with a slice of lemon. It is also often topped up with tonic or fizzy lemonade to make a longer drink. Mixed with gin, vermouth is used to make martinis.

Campari

An Italian drink flavoured with bitters, this is a popular aperitif and usually served with ice and soda.

Pimm's

A mixture of spirits, this drink is topped up with lemonade and served with ice and lemon, orange and cucumber slices. Mint sprigs are also added to make a long aperitif. There is more than one type of Pimm's and the mixture of spirits varies accordingly.

Whisky

This spelling denotes Scotch whisky, which is distilled from barley or other grain. Malt whisky is made from the malted grain. There is a wide variety of whisky, varying in flavour and quality, and forming something of a serious hobby with connoisseurs.

Whisky may be served straight, with ice, soda water or still water; it is best to offer the water separately so that it can be added to taste. Although even a moderate connoisseur will choke at the very thought, whisky is also drunk with lemonade; however, it would be a waste to treat a fine-flavoured malt whisky in this way.

Whiskey

This is the Irish drink, and the American spirit too, bourbon being one of the most famous varieties of the American whiskeys.

Gin

A spirit flavoured with juniper, gin is usually drunk with tonic on ice and with a slice of lemon. Balancing the gin with the tonic so that it is neither drowned nor too dominant is a skill which is acquired with practice. Slightly less than half gin to tonic seems to do the trick, but taste varies and many people prefer a weak drink in which the flavour of the gin is largely lost.

Vodka

Vodka which is used with a mixer is flavourless and it simply lends a kick to the mixer. It may be served with fruit juice, such as orange, or with fruit cordials, such as lime. For those who like a very dry drink, vodka may be served with a little fresh lime juice, ice and a slice of lime.

Russian vodka is served neat, very cold and in small glasses which are traditionally downed in one. Caviar, dark rye bread and soured cream are almost an accompaniment for vodka in such circumstances, rather than the other way around. Polish vodkas come in many subtle flavours and these are not served with mixers. They are served very cold, in small glasses.

Rum

White rum is the type offered as an aperitif; however, it is not as popular as other spirits. It is an ingredient in a variety of cocktails and can be used to make a refreshing long drink when combined with fruit juice.

Wine as an Aperitif

Red wine is not usually served as an aperitif but white wine is popular. Dry white wines fulfil the traditional requirements, but some of the medium dry wines and very fruity wines make pleasing drinking on their own, and they are not too sweet to kill the palate before a meal. Even if you normally serve dry wines, this is a good opportunity to sample medium-dry and fruity wines, such as those from the Alsace region of France and German wines, such as the Moselles.

Champagne makes a terrific aperitif for a special occasion and it has the advantage of being perfectly suitable for serving throughout the meal too, given that you are prepared to research the subject sufficiently to procure a wine of the correct type to match your menu or, conversely, to marry the menu to the champagne. Served in limited quantity before a meal, champagne does not have to be too costly; serving it throughout a meal will stretch the purse strings.

There are many excellent sparkling wines which are far less expensive than champagne and equally acceptable as an aperitif. Look beyond the "*méthode champenoise*" labels from the French tradition to discover excellent, well-flavoured dry sparkling wines from Australia, Spain and California. Slightly sweeter sparkling wines from Germany and Italy are also an option, but it is as well to reserve the sweet sparklers for a dessert course.

Look out for the semi-sparkling frizzante wines, too. Chardonnay frizzante, for example, is flavoursome without being too sweet, and refreshingly fizzy.

Beers as an Aperitif

It is a good idea to have beer in the refrigerator as many guests may be thirsty when they first arrive. Light, good-quality lager is the usual option.

DRINKS PARTIES

A choice of red and white wine is the norm at the majority of drinks parties, often offered with a fruit cup or some form of punch. Beers, mineral water and other non-alcoholic alternatives should be available.

If you are looking to buy a couple of cases of red and white wine for a party, try to sample some bottles yourself in advance so that you can make your choice according to personal taste as well as the name and price of the product. Taking advice from a wine merchant is a good idea. Do not be shy about pointing out that you want to keep the cost at a reasonable level; anyone can buy at the upper end of the price range with reasonable confidence, but the merchant's expertise can be particularly valuable in advising you about the moderately and lower-priced alternatives.

WINES WITH FOOD

The popular rules of white with fish and chicken and red with red meat and cheese should not inhibit the knowledgeable or adventurous cook from making alternative pairings. The wine must neither dominate or destroy the flavour of the food nor be completely eclipsed by its taste. It is thus a great mistake to offer a delicate white wine to accompany a robust casserole of game, as the flavour of the wine will be lost after a small sample of the food. Similarly, it would be quite wrong to pour a full-bodied red wine with dark tannin overtones to accompany a delicate dish of poached scallops or a plate of the first asparagus of the season, as one good draught of the wine would totally overshadow the subtle taste of

the food. Whites and reds should not be dismissed as delicate and robust respectively, however, as there are examples of both types in each camp.

Wine is not usually served with a first course of soup, nor is it offered with extremely spicy meals – for which beer or cider is more suitable. Perhaps the sensible suggestion is not to present a fine-flavoured wine with a dish like curry but to offer something inexpensive, usually white and not too dry.

White Wine

Crisp, dry white wines usually complement delicate fish and seafood dishes. Stronger fish, such as grilled mackerel or sardines, and salmon cooked with a sauce, take more distinctive white wines or light red wines. Seafood dishes are often best accompanied by a light red wine.

Chicken and turkey take either white

or red, depending on the cooking method and flavourings used. Mild-flavoured cheeses, such as Brie and smooth, musty Gruyère, are well matched by fruity white wines.

Red Wine

Red wines are usually served with meat, with the more robust and full-flavoured wines reserved for well-marinated cuts and dishes dressed with rich sauces. Pork and veal, which can be less rich than lamb and beef, also take white wines, but again a lot depends on the sauces and stuffings served. Duck is definitely a bird for red wine and game birds are also accompanied by strong reds.

When serving risottos, pasta dishes, stews and braises, then consider the overall flavour of the dish before deciding on the wine. Garlic, strong herbs, tomatoes and strong cheeses may kill a white wine, whereas a medium-bodied red wine will really bring out the best in the food. Similarly, a good strong cheese such as mature Cheddar is well complemented by a rich red wine.

Dessert Wines

Sweet dishes make too great a contrast for dry wines and the result can be quite unpleasant. Many of the sweet dessert wines, such as Sauternes, are very heavy and not to everyone's liking at the end of a meal. However, less rich sweet wines complement desserts without being too rich to drink; some of the medium-sweet wines of German origin may be served. Marsala and Madeira (Sercial) may be served with dessert. If you do want to serve a dessert wine, and particularly a good one, then plan the meal around the final course to make sure that the diners feel neither too full nor that they have imbibed sufficiently by that stage in the meal.

Port may be served with cheese. It is a classic accompaniment for Stilton, particularly when a vintage or tawny port rather than a ruby wine is selected. Ruby port may be served with some desserts, if wished.

SERVING WINE

White Wine

Dry and medium-dry white wines should be served chilled. Up to 1 hour in the refrigerator is sufficient if the wine has been taken from a fairly cool place of storage. If the wine has been in a warm shop or left out on a hot summer day, then it may be chilled for slightly longer. Over-chilling white wine is a common mistake. When the wine is left in the refrigerator for several hours its flavour is completely dulled. Very sweet wines can be chilled for slightly longer than dry wines. Champagne taken from a cool place after storage can simply be placed straight in a bucket with plenty of ice and water and left for 30 minutes before drinking. To chill in the refrigerator, leave it there for up to an hour.

Unopened bottles may be placed in the freezer for 10–15 minutes only, but do not leave them for longer as the wine will be cold and flavourless.

Red Wine

The majority of red wines should be served at room temperature. This means taking the bottle from storage and leaving it to stand in a warm, but not hot, room for up to a couple of hours before opening. If the wine is placed in a very warm room, for example a busy kitchen or near a radiator, then it will probably be fine after about 45 minutes.

If you have to warm red wine in a hurry, then the best method is to stand the bottle in a bowl of hand-hot water for 10 minutes. Despite all the experts' advice to the contrary, at least you can warm the wine by these means and it is preferable to serving a chilly red.

Opening Wine

Ideally, the wine ought to be opened a while before it is served so that the air has time to get at it and to bring out the flavour to the full. Anything up to an hour is said to be suitable. In practice, this is obviously more important when dealing with better wines. Sparkling wines are opened when you are ready to pour them.

Decanting

The vast majority of wines do not need decanting. The purpose of doing this is to draw off the wine from any sediment at the bottom of the bottle. This technique need only be applied to fine old red wines which have developed a sediment – there is nothing wrong with the wine and the sediment is often an inherent sign of the quality and age of the product. Vintage ports are the classic example of wines which have to be decanted.

Wine should be decanted into a thoroughly clean and dry glass decanter. The bottle must be carried gently on its side, just as it was stored, to avoid disturbing the sediment. Tilt it carefully and pour the wine steadily. The final 1–2.5 cm/½–1 in of wine in the bottle is not poured. A special funnel may be purchased for the decanter and the dregs may be passed through a fine sieve or muslin. (Strain the leftovers from ordinary wine into a sauce to set aside for some other cooking.)

After-dinner Drinks

Brandy, port or liqueurs may be offered when coffee is served. Port may be served earlier with the cheese. There are numerous liqueurs but the following are some of the traditional ones:

SOUTHERN COMFORT Based on bourbon whiskey, this is flavoured with orange and peach.

APRICOT BRANDY Sweetened brandy flavoured with apricots.

BENEDICTINE A brandy-based liqueur which is flavoured with herbs. It takes its name from the French monastery where it originated.

CHARTREUSE A very sweet liqueur manufactured by Carthusian monks. Both green and yellow types are available.

COINTREAU Brand name for orange-flavoured liqueur.

CRÈME DE MENTHE Mint liqueur.

DRAMBUIE A Scotch whisky-based liqueur.

GRAND MARNIER Orange liqueur.

PARFAIT D'AMOUR A scented violet-flavoured liqueur of the same colour.

AN INTRODUCTION TO ETIQUETTE

*E*tiquette, the term for the rules which apply to social interaction, is an ever-evolving framework into which the majority of social activities fit and which may be called upon as a source of reference. The dramatic changes which have taken place during the last century have made deep impressions on many of the old forms of etiquette, particularly with regard to the changing role of women and their relationship with men.

ETIQUETTE

Generally, in all but the highest echelons of society, social form is infinitely more flexible than ever before and the emphasis is on good manners rather than strict observance of ancient etiquette – a subtle, yet vital, difference. Therefore, to a large extent the surviving rules are even more relevant and important. Most people check up on etiquette in relation to specific occasions, such as weddings, and there are many thorough books which deal with such subjects.

Think of this section as an opportunity to ponder the customs and courtesies which surround the whole business of entertaining and socializing in today's fast-moving world. If some of the ideas seem superficial or unnecessary, then others are equally obviously essential for the smooth running of a million and one minor occasions. All the little everyday customs we take for granted link eventually by the same framework to the more rigid rituals which apply to formal occasions. Modern manners, rarely acknowledged, yet readily accepted, are designed to ease the process of coping with our fellows in even the most difficult of situations.

INVITATIONS

Telephone Invitations

Telephone invitations are quite acceptable for informal dinner parties and other forms of entertaining. It is both practical and pleasant to confirm in writing. However, instead of sending a written note, the party-giver may ring guests a day or two before to remind them and confirm details of timing.

Invitation cards

There is a wide range of pre-printed invitation cards available from card shops to suit most occasions. Written invitations are usually sent when the event is a more formal one, such as a formal dinner party, or when the guest list is long and telephoning would not be practical.

Alternatively, use specially printed cards that show the name, address and telephone number of the host and/or hostess, and specify "RSVP" (for the French "*Répondez, s'il vous plaît*" – "Please reply"). The names of guests, and the date, time and nature of the event can then be written in by hand. This form of printed invitation card is very useful and easily adaptable for most occasions.

Invitations to Special Occasions

If invitations are issued for a special celebration, then the wording usually indicates the reason for the invitation. These may be issued by a couple or an individual.

(name) and (name)
request the pleasure of your company at
a party to celebrate their wedding anniversary
on Saturday 30th October at 8.30 pm

RSVP
(address and telephone number)

This is a standard form for wording invitations to parties and the necessary information may be substituted. For example, if there is a theme for the party then this should be written out. If a code of dress is expected, this should be written at the bottom of the invitation – "black tie" or "fancy dress (costume)". The name of the guest(s) invited is written at the top of the invitation.

Wedding Invitations

Traditionally the bride's parents host the occasion and send out invitations six weeks before the wedding. The following form of wording is usually adopted:

(names)
request the pleasure of your company
at the marriage of their daughter
(name)
to
(name)
at (location of ceremony)
on (date)
at (time)
and afterwards at (place of reception)

RSVP (to parents' address)

There are often wedding circumstances which differ from this tradition; for example, the bride and groom may be taking sole responsibility for organizing their wedding, in which case the invitation will be issued from them. Detailed publications on the subject also advise about invitations issued by divorced parents or for the remarriage of divorced individuals. Some guests may be invited only to the reception or to an evening party following the reception, in which case a different form of wording should be used from that on the invitations to the ceremony.

Addressing Invitations

Husbands and wives are traditionally addressed by the husband's forename and surname: Mr and Mrs John Smith. This is still common practice but some women find this dismissal of their individuality quite unsuitable. Although this is a safe means of addressing strangers and casual acquaintances, if you are aware of views on the subject, then it is polite to observe them and to write both first names, possibly dropping the "Mr and Mrs". If a married woman has not taken her husband's name and you are aware of this, then invitations should be addressed to both parties: Ms Joan Brown and Mr John Smith.

Good-quality writing paper and envelopes always send out a stylish message.

GREETING GUESTS

Either the host or the hostess greets the guests on their arrival. At a small, informal occasion, the one who does not open the door joins the other and the guests promptly afterwards, allowing time for leaving guests who have already arrived. The guests are relieved of their coats and drinks are offered. While one party takes the guests in to meet the rest of the company, the other organizes drinks. Introductions may not be necessary, but the host or hostess should still make some opening remark of conversation to bring the new guests into the group.

At a larger party, the host and hostess may be too busy with the gathering to spend much time with guests when they first arrive. In this case, they should be shown or told where to take their coats and allowed to look after themselves, then they should be greeted properly when they come to join the group. Drinks should be offered and introductions made to at least a few of the other guests. Always remember to let guests know where the party is gathered if it is not immediately obvious, ". . . we're out on the patio, through the living room"; clearly indicating the location of the party will ensure that guests do not feel shy about wandering down and through the house unattended after leaving their belongings.

The conventions of making introductions dictate that the man is always introduced to the woman first and the junior to the senior, either in age or status. If a couple are introduced to a group, then they should always be named as individuals, never as "Mr Smith and his wife" or "Mr and Mrs John Smith".

Introductions should not be left as bald statements of name. It is useful to make some opening remark which will offer the guests an opportunity for beginning conversation. These remarks should be general, perhaps some reference to the link between the guest and host or hostess or a comment on the journey to the event. It is not a good idea to introduce guests by their occupation, as people often want to avoid talking about their work and the mention of some professions can immediately bring about a series of unwanted queries from other (less-than-thoughtful) guests.

Party Conversations

It really is as much the duty of the guests to make an effort to participate in conversation as it is for their hosts. However, the host and/or hostess has a responsibility for keeping an eye on the progress of topics at small gatherings, particularly when the invited company do not know each other well.

If there are subjects which the host knows are likely to be controversial or cause offence to any of the guests, then it is important that they are skilfully diverted. The subject should be changed subtly and moved on in the required direction without dropping any drastic and irrelevant comments into the conversation. Sometimes, if the situation has reached a stage at which an immediate change of direction is required, the best course of action is to dismiss the previous topic completely and throw open a whole new idea more widely, picking a popular theme which is likely to be quickly expanded upon by several guests.

SEATING ARRANGEMENTS

Traditionally, the host and hostess sit at the head of the table, with the most important female guest on the right of the host, the most important male guest on the right of the hostess. Traditionally, in households where women would always be 'taken in' to dinner and where staff looked after the business of serving food, the host takes the most important female guest into dinner first, followed by the other guests and the most important man takes the hostess in to dinner last. The remaining ladies would be escorted in strict order of rank by the men, also in order of rank, and the next most important lady would sit on the left of the host, the next most important man on the left of the hostess. The remaining guests

Use small pieces of card with guests' initials on to work out a seating plan.

Serve freshly made coffee and after-dinner chocolates to round off the evening.

would fill the table in order of rank away from the hosts, with men and women occupying alternate seats.

Modern dinner parties are often smaller and definitely less complicated. Since the majority of hostesses prepare the food and they are usually helped by their partners when serving, even the tradition of their taking the head places at table is waived since many dining rooms are too small for the host to leave his seat discreetly, pass all the guests and absent himself to assist with serving the meal without causing chaos. Therefore the host and hostess may sit together at one end of the table but the tradition of alternating male and female guests is usually observed and partners are often split to encourage conversation.

Men should wait until the women are seated before taking their places and it is still courteous, if space allows, for a man to hold the chair for his female neighbour.

SERVING FOOD AT DINNER

Women are served first. Men assist the women by offering them vegetable dishes and so on. It is also courteous for women to do the same.

Guests are not expected to wait until the hostess has served all the company before they begin to serve themselves with vegetables, as this only causes delay and allows the food to become cold. It is quite correct for guests to begin eating before all are served, though it is not necessarily considerate. It is more helpful if guests who have served themselves with accompaniments are ready to assist in passing plates or dishes. However, they should begin once it is clear that everyone is about to be served and their help is no longer useful.

The host usually pours the first glass of wine and it is his responsibility to keep an eye on glasses and to refill them as necessary. Often, particularly at larger dinner parties, the guests are invited to serve themselves from bottles distributed on the table. It is polite for guests to offer to top up their neighbours' glasses, particularly for men to look after women.

After Dinner

Coffee may be served at the table or in the living room. The choice is entirely up to the host or hostess. Moving from the table can break up a dinner party which is going very well, in which case it is best to allow conversation to flow and to serve the coffee and liqueurs at the table.

Liqueurs should be set out at one side so that guests can see what is offered, or they may be offered by name. Port and brandy may be placed on the table. If smoking is welcomed, then guests may be invited to take

cigars; however, this is far less common these days.

Traditionally, the women left the table at a nod from the hostess (to the chief female guest) and departed to the drawing room for coffee. The men then indulged in port or brandy and cigars for a period of 15 minutes before joining the ladies – although the rules of etiquette clearly advised the men should not linger longer, it is difficult to believe that they abandoned their port so quickly.

If coffee is taken elsewhere it should be set out before the guests leave the table, then they should be invited to move by the host or hostess.

TAKING LEAVE

Guests leaving a large party should seek out either the host or hostess to say goodbye, unless they are leaving early, when this can be disruptive. Usually a guest who has to leave early should let the host know on arrival, if not beforehand.

After a dinner party, the host and hostess should see the guests to the door, helping them with their coats, then speedily return to remaining guests and encourage conversation if the dinner party is to continue.

CHILDREN

When you invite couples who have children you must decide whether the children are invited or not and make it clear on the invitation, either by including their names or by naming the couple and excluding the children.

You should be prepared for guests who may double-check that their children are not invited. Do not allow yourself to be cornered into inviting one set of children, as this will cause offence to other couples whose families have not been invited. Try to make as little as possible of the fact by simply saying that on this occasion it is an adults-only party. However, it is worth remembering that unless there is a good reason for making it an adults-only event, then many couples may have difficulties in finding someone to care for their children.

If children are included, do make plans for them as well as for other guests. Do not include them on the invitations simply with the intention of ignoring them – think in terms of the food and drinks they are likely to consume, special plates and plastic tumblers, entertainments and so on.

Helping Guests to Leave

There is no easy way of dismissing guests who are lingering longer than required. Allowing conversation to lapse at the end of a dinner party is a good way of indicating that you want guests to leave and this should be accompanied by gentle yawning, with comment on how busy you have been or how tired you are.
❖ Blow out candles which are getting conveniently short to indicate that the party is over. Allow a fire to burn very low, saying, ". . . it's not worth putting another log on now".
❖ Comments about plans for the next morning, especially if an early start is involved, may work.
❖ It may be time to start doing the washing up – there's nothing like the crashing of crockery to break up a dinner party.
❖ At worst, try asking about last trains/taxis/the length of the drive home/whether the car starts well on cold evenings and other pointed topics on transport.
❖ As a last resort, clear away the cups and return with the coats: ". . . I thought I'd bring these in since you were just about to get them; it's draughty in our hallway so you may like to put them on here. It has been lovely to see you again."

Standing Place Cards

Place cards are always laid at formal or large dinners. Simple, elegant cards are best for such occasions. Lay them in a suitable position on the setting, such as on a side plate or with the napkin.

YOU WILL NEED: card (posterboard); (for making stencil) paper, pencil, sticky (transparent) tape; craft knife, stencil or sheet of acetate, waterproof black felt-tip pen, gold paint, stencil brush, thin coloured ribbon.

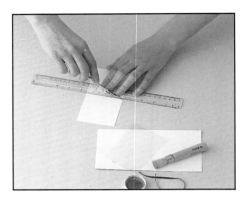

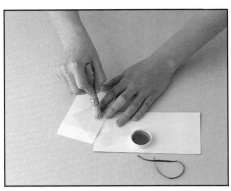

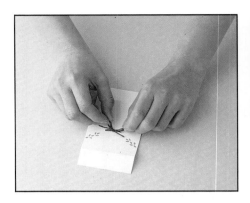

1 Cut a strip of card (posterboard) measuring 15 × 7.5 cm/6 × 3 in. Mark a fold across the centre of the card and a 2.5 cm/1 in fold at each end of the strip. Lightly score the folds with a craft knife, but be careful not to cut through the card.

2 If you are making your own stencil, draw your design onto a sheet of paper. Place the sheet of acetate on top and tape in position to hold the sheet firmly in place. Transfer the design to the acetate using a waterproof black felt-tip pen. Cut around the outline of the design using the craft knife. Lightly load the brush with gold paint. Holding the stencil firmly in position, press the brush over the pattern in the stencil keeping the brush vertical.

3 To attach the ribbon, mark and then cut two small slits in the card. Thread the ribbon through and tie into a bow. Trim the ends of the ribbon if necessary.

Cut-out Place Cards

Use patterned card (posterboard) for these attractive place cards: special marbled, coloured, gold or silver card is suitable.

YOU WILL NEED: plain card, patterned card, tracing paper, pencil, craft knife, glue.

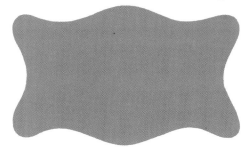

1 For each place card, you will need a strip of patterned card (posterboard) measuring 20 × 10 cm/8 × 4 in. Trace the pattern for the cut-out area onto tracing paper. Using a soft pencil, shade the area underneath the tracing. Mark a fold across the centre of the card and a 2.5 cm/1 in fold at each end of the strip. Lightly score the folds with a craft knife, but do not cut through the card. Lay the tracing shaded side down on the reverse of one half of the patterned card, positioned centrally. Using a sharp pencil, follow the line of the design.

2 On a hard surface, use the craft knife to cut out the shape.

3 Push the cut-out area from the right side of the card, *not* from the back. Take care to push out any intricate designs carefully.

4 Cut out a strip of plain card measuring 9.5 × 7 cm/3¾ × 2¾ in. Stick the plain card behind the cut-out area on the patterned card with glue.

NAPKIN ART

*C*risp, *freshly laundered napkins are an essential feature of every well-set table. They may be pressed in large, plain squares and laid at each place with the minimum of fuss and for the maximum effect. Alternatively, they may be* *folded in a variety of ways to complement the food, table layout and occasion. Try some of the ideas in the following pages and use them as a source of inspiration for developing your own individual napkin art.*

PERFECT NAPKINS

Regardless of the simplicity of the meal, fabric napkins must be spotlessly clean and well pressed.

❖ Plain white linen napkins may be embroidered by hand or by machine with a monogram of your initials. This may be surrounded by a wreath of leaves or some other decorative embroidery. Fold monogrammed napkins very simply to display the embroidery.

❖ Press embroidered napkins on the wrong side to make the pattern stand out attractively.

❖ Decorative napkins, trimmed with embroidery or lace or with a prominent self pattern, should be folded very simply; plain fabric napkins or those with a small decorative border are more suitable for elaborate folding.

Paper Napkins

Paper napkins are more practical than fabric ones for parties. Choose those that are large, absorbent and fairly thick; the thin, small paper napkins that disintegrate easily are more hindrance than help. The exception to this rule is Japanese paper napkins.

BRIGHT PAPER NAPKINS For fun parties use a selection of different coloured paper napkins: pastels or primary colours both work well. Fold them in half, then overlap them in a large basket and fold one napkin into a water lily shape for the centre of the arrangement.

Paper napkins are a practical option for informal barbecues, especially when sticky spareribs and other finger foods are served. When laying a garden table, allow two or three different coloured napkins for each place setting. They may be fanned out simply or pairs of contrasting colours used double for folding shapes such as a water lily or roll-top design.

JAPANESE PAPER NAPKINS Look out for fine paper napkins which are very thin but quite strong. They are often delicately patterned and may be round or square, with fluted or gilded edges. As well as being used on their own, they may be used in conjunction with linen napkins for courses which are eaten with the fingers as part of a formal meal, especially when finger bowls are provided. Fold them attractively with the linen napkins, then clear the paper napkins away after they have been used.

NAPKINS FOR BUFFETS

If you are preparing a buffet for a comparatively small number, that is, under fifteen guests, then it is a good idea to use linen napkins if possible. The fabrics do not have to be the same and a virtue can be made of their differences by combining contrasting colours or patterns in an attractive arrangement.

❖ For larger gatherings or when there are lots of children around, it is an advantage to have lots of spare paper napkins to deal with any spills. Bear in mind that guests rarely retain their napkins after the main course and many may take a second for dessert.

❖ Elaborate folding methods are not used for buffet presentation as the emphasis is mainly on the practicalities of carrying a plate, napkin and cutlery (flatware). There are a number of standard options for placing napkins.

❖ Roll a knife and fork in a napkin. If the number of guests is small and space on the buffet table limited, the cutlery and napkins may be fanned out attractively, near the plates. It is often more practical to pile them in a basket, or two, and place them near the plates or on a separate side table with condiments or bread. Do not roll cutlery for

A tartan bow holds a neatly rolled napkin and spoon for a dessert course.

dessert in the napkin; this should be offered separately.

❖ Stack a napkin on each plate.

❖ Fold the napkins in half diagonally to make triangles and overlap these on one side of the buffet table.

❖ Roll the napkins and stand them in a wide jug or arrange them in a basket.

TIPS FOR SUCCESSFUL FOLDING

For folding purposes, heavy linen is best, as it becomes firm and crisp when starched. Plain dinner napkins measuring 45–50 cm/18–20 in square, or more, are best and are essential for many complicated folding techniques.

❖ The napkins must be cut square and the fabric must be cut straight on the weave so that the napkins will not pull out of shape easily.

❖ Linen should be washed, starched with traditional starch (spray starch will not give a sufficiently crisp finish) and ironed while damp. When ironing, gently pull the napkins back into shape if necessary to ensure they are perfectly square again.

❖ It is best to iron napkins on a large surface; an ironing board can be too narrow when pressing large napkins. Protect the surface with a folded thick towel, which should be covered with a piece of plain white cotton.

❖ Dampen napkins which have dried before ironing. Traditional starch may be mixed and sprayed on linen using a clean plant spray. Allow it to soak into

the fabric for a minute or so before ironing for best results.

When folding napkins into complicated shapes, press each fold individually for best results. Soft folds should not be pressed.

SIMPLE PRESENTATION

To form a neat square, press the napkin, making sure all the corners are perfectly square. Fold it into quarters, pressing each fold. A large quarter-folded napkin may be laid square between the cutlery (flatware) at each place or it may be turned by ninety degrees. This is fine on large tables.

❖ To make a simple triangle, fold the square in half diagonally and press the resulting triangle neatly. Lay the triangular-folded napkin on a side plate, with the long side nearest the place setting. The triangle may also be laid on top of a plate in the middle of the setting.

❖ For a simple oblong, fold a square napkin in half again. This is an ideal way of displaying a decorative corner on the napkin. Plain napkins may be folded and pressed into quarters, then the sides folded underneath and pressed to make an oblong shape. Lay the hemmed edge on the short side at the bottom of the place setting.

❖ Rolled napkins may be kept in place with napkin rings or tied with ribbon or cord. If the napkins are rolled carefully and laid with the end underneath, they will usually sit quite neatly.

Place Mat

A large, square, cloth napkin can be used as a pretty place mat.

1 Fold the four corners into the centre.

2 Place a hand over the middle to hold the corners in position and turn the napkin over.

3 Fold all four corners of the napkin into the centre again and carefully turn the napkin over for a second time.

4 Fold each centre corner back to meet the outside corner, and press.

Bishop's Hat

This is a very traditional method of folding large dinner napkins. The proportions are important, so it may be necessary to adjust some of the folds as you work it through.

1 Starting with the corners of the open napkin top and bottom in the form of a diamond, fold the corner nearest to you to just below the corner furthest away from you to form a triangle.

2 Fold up the two corners nearest to you until the edges align.

3 Bring the newly created bottom corner up and away from you so that its top edge sits just below the first corner when folded.

4 Fold down the front edge.

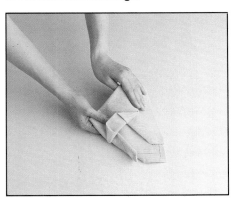

5 Bend the left and right corners backwards and interlock one half into the other to form a tube that will not spring open.

Spreading Fan

An elegant yet simple design that is
suitable for all occasions.

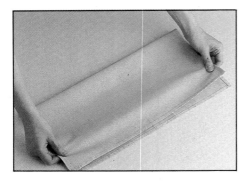

1 Fold up the edge nearest to you to meet the
top edge.

2 Rotate the napkin so that the folded edge is
on your right. Make equal-sized accordian
pleats all the way up to the top of the napkin,
starting with the edge nearest to you.

3 Insert the napkin into the ring, or tie with
ribbon or cord and spread out the pleats.

Water Lily

This design requires a well-starched napkin to make the cup shape. It can be used to hold a bread roll, a small gift or seasonal decorations such as small fir cones and holly at Christmas, chocolate hearts for Valentine's Day, or a tiny posy of spring flowers.

1 Fold the corners of the napkin into the centre and press flat.

2 Repeat the process a second time.

3 Holding the centre points together, carefully turn the napkin over.

4 Fold the four corners into the centre again, but do not press.

5 Holding the centre firmly, partly pull out the previous fold from under each corner and gently pull them upward to make the petals.

6 Pull out the corners from underneath between the petals, to form the base leaves of the lily.

FLOWERS FOR ALL OCCASIONS

*F*lowers are the most popular of centrepieces and decorations for any party occasion, from a simple bowl of daisies on a kitchen table to a breathtaking arrangement for a buffet table or a reception area. This section can only hint at the variety of designs that can be achieved for home entertaining, but it will provide a source of inspiration and ideas for inexperienced flower arrangers who want to experiment with traditional arrangements.

As well as fresh flowers, remember to make the most of the wide range of foliage and dried and preserved flowers available. The advantage of preserved material is that the arrangements can be prepared well ahead of a party without any need for time-consuming last-minute attention.

Finally, do not underestimate the time needed to create complex decorations. Swags, wreaths and garlands all look beautiful, but they cannot be put together in minutes. Always prepare as much as possible in advance, leaving only the finishing touches to be done on the day.

Foam bases, and fixing and decorative material.

BASIC EQUIPMENT

Take full advantage of the many items of equipment that are readily available at garden centres and florists, as they make life easier even when trying to prepare a simple bowl of flowers for an informal table centrepiece.

Bases

FOAM BASES These are the most practical, as they can be cut to any shape and size required. They come in two basic forms: dry foam (styro foam), which is used for dried and preserved flowers, and wet foam, which has to be soaked and is used for fresh flowers.

HEAVY SPIKED BASE A heavy spiked base may be used to hold a foam base, lending it weight and stability. This is particularly useful for arrangements of dried flowers, which tend to be light.

Conceal wire stems with floral tape.

Containers

Almost anything can be used as a container for flowers, from formal cut-glass vases and ceramic vessels to pots, jugs and bowls. Waterproof containers must be used for fresh flowers. If you want to disguise a container, consider placing it inside a basket or swathing it in fabric.

Florists' wire

This is available ready-cut and in various gauges. Fine wire is suitable for delicate flowers and for paper tissue or crêpe paper flowers. Thicker wire is required for wiring foliage and sturdy stems. Don't worry if, as is sometimes the case, the packet or bundle of wires does not specify the gauge. By comparing the different wires, it is fairly obvious which types are suitable for the flowers to be arranged. Plastic-covered wire used for the garden is also extremely useful for all sorts of craft tasks, such as making garlands. You will need wire cutters and fine pliers for cutting and twisting wire.

Bases for Wreaths

Circular bases for wreaths are available ready-made in rigid foam (styro foam) or cane (willow).

Cane rings are ideal for arrangements using heavy foliage and large blooms, and the canework is decorative enough to be treated as part of the overall finished look, and not completely disguised.

Rigid foam rings are better for flowery wreaths made from dried, silk or fresh flowers. Fresh flowers must be left up to their necks in water overnight and wired just before they are used, otherwise they will not look their best.

Trim off excess foliage and shoots before arranging.

PREPARING PLANT MATERIAL

Trim excess leaves and side shoots which will get in the way of an arrangement. Snip the ends off the stems of flowers and foliage which have been cut for some time or have been bought. With a heavy object, crush or slit the ends of firm stems, such as the stems of roses and carnations. Place the materials up to their necks in a bucket of water in the shade for several hours before arranging them. Rinse and dust foliage and shake out flower heads, as they often contain insects which can creep out on the dining table only to make their social debut at one of your most important dinner parties!

Wiring Flowers and Foliage

For posies and floral sprays, especially for decorating swags on tablecloths and for wiring into wreaths or garlands, it may be necessary to cut off the stem 5 cm/2 in from the flower. Bend the end of the wire into a small hook. Thread the straight end down through the flower head and into the stem so that the hook catches firmly in place. This is suitable for flowers such as chrysanthemums. Alternatively, push the wire through the stem as far as the flower head, then twist it gently around the stem to hold the wire in place. Cover the wires and flower stems with florists' tape. This method is also useful for any floppy foliage.

Crush thick woody stems with a heavy object.

Balls and Bells

An arrangement does not have to be limited to flowers, foliage and ribbon. Give your imagintion a little freedom when you look around craft shops and stores, particularly at Christmas time, as there are lots of exciting materials which may be used in centrepieces.

GLASS BALLS These come in all sorts of colours that are far removed from the traditional Christmas colours. Peachy pinks, dusky mauves, pearly whites and lemon yellows are just a few examples of the opaque balls that can be found. They add an interesting and attractive dimension to corner decorations for tables as well as to flower ropes and garlands.

BELLS Similarly, some of the beautiful glass bells and slippers which are readily available at Christmas, and which can also be found in specialist craft or sugarcraft stores the rest of the year, have a place among floral decorations. Bells are ideal for silver and golden wedding anniversaries as well as weddings. Slippers are considered to be a charm for good fortune in some countries, and are frequently seen on wedding cakes and incorporated into floral decorations.

SHAPING AN ARRANGEMENT

It is important to decide on the shape of the arrangement to suit the table and the materials used. The finished arrangement should look well balanced from all sides and this can only be achieved if you plan the outline first.

Place the first pieces of foliage or buds at the extremities of the arrangement so that the outline is clearly established. These should have firm lines to give definition to the shape.

Next, place a bloom or foliage at the required highest point of the arrangement – this does not necessarily have to be the centre, as the design may slope in a tear-drop shape. However, remember to consider the table when planning this shape – an off-centre high point may look good towards one corner of a buffet table, for example, but it could look strange from either end of a dining table.

Once you have established the key points, gradually build up the shape of the arrangement, working all around and from the base. Never allow the arrangement to extend beyond the length, width and height set by the first pieces of material or you will lose the overall structure and balance.

Do not fill up the arrangement completely from the base. Once you have sufficient material to see a clear shape, fill in from the top of the arrangement and from the sides.

Remember to balance the size of blooms to the shape of the arrangement. Place larger flowers in the middle – or two or three key blooms in a smaller decoration – then work down in size as you move out.

Gaps and hollows should be filled as appropriate. Always stand well back from an arrangement and walk all around it to check the shape. Sometimes it helps to go away for 15 minutes, then come back and look at the arrangement with a fresh eye.

BOWLS OF FLOWERS

Not all arrangements have to be stiff and formal, even for important occasions. Looser arrangements often look charming, but they still need a little attention. Select a pretty bowl or small low flower holder and place a piece of wet foam in the base. If the flower holder already comes with a glass base with holes for stems, position a piece of foam on top or cover the base with a small piece of crumpled chicken wire. The holes are rarely designed for the flowers you use or the shape you want!

Gradually build up the arrangement, making sure it looks attractive on all sides. You may want to cover the container completely, in which case choose curved or dropping shapes that will naturally fall down over it. To avoid ending up with a stiff round shape, make sure you always bring some greenery or material down over the edge of the container in a few places, to soften the shape.

Yellow and Peach Table Centrepiece

When working on a table arrangement to be seen from all sides, it's a good idea to keep viewing it from different angles to make sure that it looks equally good all round. This oval arrangement is asymmetrical but evenly balanced.

YOU WILL NEED: a container, a block of wet florists' foam, flowers and foliage (wired as necessary), ribbon loops.

1 Establish the overall width and length of the arrangement using sprays of leaves as a foundation. Next place three or five flower sprays at key points to create the outline shape and height.

2 Fill in the central shape using clustered heads of tiny flowers.

3 Position larger shapely flower heads to add drama, maintaining the overall shape. Insert smaller flowers and ribbon bows to finish.

Cushion Posy

Neat and charming, this little dome-shaped arrangement takes up very little space.

YOU WILL NEED: a container, a cylinder of wet florists' foam, flowers and foliage (wired as necessary), ribbon loops.

1 Establish the basic outline with a radiating arrangement of foliage. Position key flowers symmetrically around the perimeter and in the centre to show the highest point. Add leaves between the flowers at the edges.

2 Fill in the gaps with smaller blooms, clusters of tiny flowers and ribbon loops, maintaining the overall domed shape.

Ribbon Loops

Ribbon loops in toning colours enhance any flower arrangement. Make sure the ribbon is stiff enough to hold a loop without flopping. Choose wide or narrow ribbon, and experiment with loops of different sizes to suit the proportions of the arrangement.

YOU WILL NEED: stiff florists' ribbon, scissors, fine florists' wire.

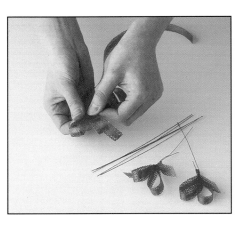

1 Fold the ribbon into pairs of loops of the required length. Trim off excess ribbon.

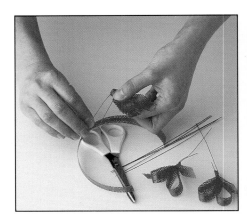

2 Holding the loops near the base between thumb and forefinger, make two small snips towards the centre through all layers of ribbon. Twist wire around the ribbon in the snips to secure the loops. Push the end of the wire into the arrangement.

Wired Bows

Wired bows are quick to make and can be scaled up to any size by using wider ribbon, or even paper.

YOU WILL NEED: ribbon, scissors, fine florists' wire.

1 Fold the ribbon into a bow shape and hold the crossover between thumb and forefinger. Twist a length of wire around the middle to hold in shape.

2 Make a small loop in the ribbon to hide the join. Secure with wire, then cut off excess ribbon.

Hanging Spherical Posy

The charm of this pretty posy is its perfect ball shape. It is sometimes easiest to hang it by its ribbon when adding the flowers to the underside.

YOU WILL NEED: a dry florists' foam (styro foam) sphere, florists' ribbon, florists' wire, scissors, flowers.

1 Make a hanging loop from florists' ribbon and secure the ends with a length of wire. Push the end of the wire through the foam sphere.

2 Bend the end of the wire back towards the sphere to prevent it from slipping out.

3 Wire individual blooms and trim the wires to about 2.5–3.5 cm/1–1½ in. Push the wired stems into the foam to cover it evenly.

4 Make little bundles of smaller flower heads, wire them in the same way and insert them between the larger blooms.

Flower Basket

A wide range of wicker baskets and trugs frame flower arrangements attractively, but freestanding wire baskets make subtle containers that allow the flowers to speak for themselves.

YOU WILL NEED: basket with wet florists' foam base to fit, sphagnum moss, flowers, trailing ivy, reindeer moss, florists' wire, scissors.

1 Stand the soaked florists' foam base in the wire basket on a plate to catch any drips. Cover the top and sides with damp sphagnum moss.

2 Select two or three flower heads of similar toning colours and arrange them attractively.

3 Wire the flowers together into little bunches.

4 Push the wired flower stems into the foam base, working around the outer edge.

5 Insert single ivy leaves here and there between the flowers.

6 Wind trails of ivy around the perimeter between the flower heads, pushing the ends firmly down into the foam base.

7 Fill the centre with wired tufts of reindeer moss to create a high domed shape.

Spiky Paper Flowers

Use paper of a single colour for each bloom, or make each layer from a different shade — for example, from pink through mauve and violet to blue — for a glowing, luminous effect. Crêpe paper makes suitably chunky leaves to contrast with the delicate flowers.

YOU WILL NEED: 20 cm/8 in squares of tissue paper in flower colours and crêpe paper in green, florists' wire, small paper scissors, needle.

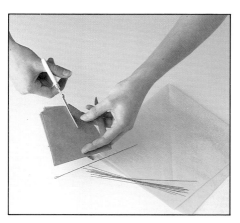

1 Bend a small loop in one end of a length of wire. Fold four sheets of tissue paper together into quarters. Beginning about 2.5 cm/1 in away from the central corner, cut a circle of spikes radiating out towards the outer edges of the paper.

2 Open out the folds and use a needle to make a hole through the centre. Push the straight end of the wire through the hole. Separate the tissue paper layers and rotate them slightly to stagger them.

3 Turn the flower over and gently gather the petals over the wire loop. Holding the bottom of the flower between thumb and forefinger, twist the wire two or three times around the centre of the paper to secure.

4 Fold the sheets of crêpe paper in half and cut out leaf shapes. Wire these in the same way and arrange between and around the flowers.

Flower Rope

A single flower rope adds decoration to an awkward panel of wall — beside a door for example. A pair looks elegant framing a fireplace. Alternatively, a series of ropes can be suspended at links in paper chains or swags of ribbon. Hung from table edges, they create a very festive atmosphere.

YOU WILL NEED: green raffia, florists' wire, florists' tape, pins, flower heads such as orchids, lilies etc, foliage such as ivy, ruscus etc, narrow and wide matching ribbon.

1 Tie a knot at one end of the bundle of raffia, divide the strands into three and plait (braid) loosely. Trim the end to length and secure.

2 Make a loop at one end of a length of florists' wire and wire individual ivy leaves.

3 Hold an ivy leaf and an orchid together and twist the wire around both stems. Bind both stems together with florists' tape.

4 Wire and tape together other flower heads and leaves. Insert an orchid and ivy leaf near the top of the raffia rope.

5 Insert a second wired flower head into the raffia rope below the orchid, positioning it at an attractive angle to add width.

6 Continue to add further flower heads and leaves, alternating the angles to achieve a balanced effect. Position one flower head to conceal the end of the raffia rope.

7 Wind a trail of ruscus leaves around the raffia rope, tucking it in behind the flowers. Make little long-tailed bows with narrow ribbon, and curl the ends.

8 Attach the little bows to the raffia with pins. Arrange a spray of ivy to add width at the top of the rope and wire in place. Attach a large ribbon bow at the top.

Herb Cone

Many aromatic-leaved herbs will last well out of water to make an unusual focal point. Contrast their foliage textures with the warm tones of spices, and add ribbon bows in a harmonizing colour. For best results, crush the ends of the herb stems and stand them in water for 12 hours before beginning.

YOU WILL NEED: a cone-shaped dry florists' foam (styro foam) form, herbs such as rosemary, bay and thyme, pins, florists' wire, spices such as whole cloves and cinnamon sticks, ribbon bows, raffia, reindeer moss, a plate.

1 Working downwards, pin bay leaves to the cone. Overlap the leaves and position in a spiralling shape, wider at the base than the top.

2 Cut short lengths of florists' wire and bend them into hooks. Cut short sprigs of rosemary.

3 Use the wire hooks to pin sprigs of rosemary to the cone, following the spiralling curve of the bay leaves.

4 Attach a spiralling line of thyme sprigs to the cone in the same way. Pack cloves tightly together to infill the spaces between the herbs. Place the covered cone on a plate. Surround the base with tufts of reindeer moss, ribbon bows and bundles of cinnamon sticks tied with raffia.

Miniature Vegetable Garland

Choose colourful, shapely whole vegetables such as baby carrots, small onions, artichokes and aubergines (eggplants) and chilli peppers, and mix them with florets (flowerets) of broccoli and sprigs of herbs for contrast. The plaited (braided) raffia is easy to hang as a garland but also looks good simply laid on the table.

YOU WILL NEED: raffia, florists' wire, darning needle (optional), small vegetables, sprigs of herbs, twisted paper ribbon.

1 Plait (braid) three bundles of raffia together loosely to make a rope of the required length. Secure the ends with a strand of raffia.

2 Wire the vegetables individually. Use a darning needle to pierce holes for the wires if necessary, or wrap wires securely around the stalks.

3 Wire little bundles of vegetables together. Insert the wire through to the back of the raffia and secure inconspicuously there.

4 Wire little bunches of herbs together. Wire these into the raffia in between the vegetables.

5 Untwist a length of ribbon for a bow. To make the loops, fold the ends to the centre and staple in place.

6 Wrap a second length of ribbon around the centre of the bow, leaving the ends dangling as tails. Staple in place. Make a second bow in the same way. Fold the ends of the raffia rope under to neaten, tie with raffia and trim. Attach a ribbon bow to either end with wire.

Miniature Vegetable Garland.

Garlands

Garlands can be long and made from flexible material, such as raffia or twisted paper, and hung across · walls, tables, down staircases and so on, or keep them short for placing above mirrors or doorways.

LONG FLEXIBLE GARLANDS

Measure the length you require – if the garland is for a swagged tablecloth you may prefer to make a series of individual garlands to string between each swag. The raffia or twisted paper needs to be plaited (braided) first, so you will need three lengths, each one slightly longer than the required length. Tie a knot at one end of the raffia or twisted paper and plait (braid) loosely. Trim the end to length and secure. Fold the rope in half and mark the lowest, or mid-point in the sweep. Wire the decorative material, then thread it through the

garland, always ensuring that everything faces the mid-point. Secure the material at the back of the garland. Finish by securing a trio of flowers with leaves at the mid-point. Secure a wire loop at each end of the garland for fixing in position if necessary.

SHORT GARLANDS

Prepare a base as before measuring 50–60 cm/20–24 in long. If you want to add large items to the garland, such as large cones and sprays of holly, the base must be at least 5 cm/2 in wide. Run a double thickness of sturdy tying wire through the base so that it can be easily curved into a neat shape that will hold its form before adding any decoration. Add a wire loop at each end as before for fixing. Begin by wiring in key material, such as large flowers or cones, then fill in the gaps with background material. Stop and check as you go along that the arrangement is well balanced.

Add bows at the ends to conceal the wire loops.

CHAIN GARLANDS

Chain garlands are made by forming interlocking rings made from raffia or twisted paper, which comes in a variety of colours. A length of about 35 cm/14 in should be prepared for each link in the chain and secured in a circle. When one circle is formed, the next length is threaded through it before being secured. It is best to secure two or three links at a time, then wire the decorative material onto these before adding the next few links and so on. Lay out the chain on a long flat surface or on the floor as you work up the chain.

Remember to secure hanging wire loops at the ends and at points where the chain will be strung up. These may be concealed with bows and trailing ribbon ends in appropriate colours.

Special Occasions

THE ART OF FOOD PRESENTATION

The first all-important impression of many a dish is a visual one, so it is essential to create a tempting appearance which stirs up a sense of anticipation for the delights to follow. Regardless of the simplicity or sophistication of a *recipe, there is no excuse for less-than-perfect presentation. This brief section runs through some practical points on preparing and serving dishes for the table, and ideas for garnishing and decorating a range of foods.*

SIMPLE RULES FOR SERVING

There are a few basic rules of food presentation that are practical, as well as decorative. These are the first steps in ensuring that food arrives at the table looking appealing.

❖ Oven-to-table dishes must be in good condition. Always clean the outside of dishes and the rims before taking them to the table. Take care, however, not to crack a hot dish by wiping it with a wet cloth. Clean up the dish during the cooking process to avoid any baked-on residue.

❖ Plates should be warmed before serving hot food.

❖ If soup is served, try not to slop it about in the bowl on the way to the table as this creates an unattractive tide mark on the side of the bowl.

❖ If a cold first course is plated in advance, do not leave it to dry out before serving; keep each plate covered with cling film (plastic wrap).

❖ If the main course is plated and sauced before being taken to the table, always wipe away any small drips or spills before presenting the dish.

❖ When serving the main course at the table, plan one that is easy to carve or serve, or be prepared to cope with the problem in advance. For example, it may be prudent to slice or cut up the food in the kitchen before taking it to the table to serve.

❖ Food which is meant to be served hot should be just that; chilled food should be left in the refrigerator until just before it is served.

A GUIDE TO GARNISHING

The garnish should fulfil two functions: to complement the ingredients in a dish and to make it look pretty. Recipes often specify a particular garnish for these reasons, one that is integral to the dish, not merely an afterthought. Garnishes don't have to be fancy or complicated to achieve the desired effect – adding a sprig of dill to a fish dish, for example, often completes the picture and will add to the flavour. However, do avoid the ubiquitous lettuce leaf and tomato quarter if at all possible.

Useful Cutting Techniques

CANELLE STRIPS Use a special canelle knife to pare long, fine strips of skin or rind (peel) along the whole length of cucumbers, oranges or lemons. This produces a decorative cog-wheel effect when the vegetable or fruit is then sliced.

The pared strips of lemon or orange rind can also be used as a garnish if they are simmered first in water until tender, then drained well on absorbent kitchen paper (paper towels).

JULIENNE STRIPS Also known as julienne, these are matchstick-thin strips, usually cut from vegetables such as carrots, celeriac (celery root), celery, turnips, white radish and courgettes (zucchini). First cut the vegetables into thin slices and neaten the ends, then cut the slices into short, very thin strips.

VEGETABLE SHAPES Thinly slice carrots, potatoes, celeriac (celery root) or swede (rutabaga). Cook the slices in boiling water until just tender, then drain well. Use aspic cutters to stamp out shapes. Use this attractive garnish for chaudfroid dishes, terrines, aspic-coated foods and mousses.

Salad Garnish

Prepare these spring onion (green onion) curls in advance and set them aside in a covered bowl in the refrigerator to keep them crisp and fresh. Add to the plates at the last minute. This is a particularly effective garnish on Chinese-style dishes.

1 Shred the green part of an onion, leaving all the strips attached at the bulb end.

2 Place in a bowl of iced water for at least 30 minutes in the refrigerator and the shredded part will curl. Drain well on absorbent kitchen paper (paper towels).

Fleurons

These are small crescent shapes of puff pastry. They are delicious served with soups, sauced dishes and other savoury foods that are enhanced by a contrasting crisp texture.

Roll out the pastry (dough) thinly and use a crescent-shaped cutter to cut out the shapes. Brush each shape carefully with a little beaten egg and place them on a damp baking sheet. Bake at 220°C/425°F/Gas 7 for about 10 minutes, until well puffed and golden. Cool on a wire rack.

Melba Toast

Serve melba toast with pâtés and savoury mousses. The toast will keep for several weeks stored in an airtight container.

Lightly toast medium-sliced bread on both sides under a hot grill (broiler). Remove from the grill and cut off the crusts. Using a sharp knife, cut through the centre of the toast to form two thin slices. Place the untoasted side face upwards on the grill pan and toast until golden brown.

CARROT FLOWERS Peel a carrot, then cut thin strips out of the side, working lengthways. When the carrot is sliced, the slices will have decorative edges. Blanch in boiling water until tender before use.

VANDYKE CUTTING Use this technique to give tomatoes, lemons, oranges, limes and radishes a fancy edge. Cut around the middle of the fruit with a small, fine-bladed knife, cutting a zig-zag pattern and in as far as the middle of the fruit. When cuts are made all around, pull the two halves apart to reveal the decorative zig-zag surfaces.

Bread and Pastry Garnishes

CROÛTONS Cut thinly sliced bread into small shapes, such as dice, triangles and small circles. Heat a mixture of butter, olive oil and garlic (optional) until sizzling hot, then fry the croûtons until golden brown all over. Drain well on absorbent kitchen paper (paper towels). You can make these in advance and store in an airtight container. Sprinkle on soups and salads.

CROÛTES These are pieces of fried bread larger than croûtons, which are served around a casserole or under

portions of fried food, such as steaks, to absorb the juices. Prepare as for croûtons. Store in an airtight container

PHYLLO FLAKES A good way of using up broken or slightly dry sheets of phyllo pastry. Snip the pastry into small irregular shaped pieces, then place on a thoroughly greased baking sheet. Trickle a little oil evenly over the pastry. Bake at 180°C/350°F/Gas 4 for 20–30 minutes turning the pieces occasionally. The cooking time depends on how much pastry is on the baking sheet and the thickness of the layer. Use hot or cold as a crunchy topping.

73

Marbling

This is a technique for decorating sauces and soups, combining soft mixtures which will be left to set.

Flood a plate with a dark, coloured sauce, such as a chocolate or fruit sauce. Trickle a little cream at random over the sauce. Use the point of a fine metal skewer to drag the cream through the sauce, swirling it to achieve an attractive marble effect. Alternatively, use a pale custard sauce with a contrasting dark sauce to make the marbling.

Feathering

An alternative to marbling.

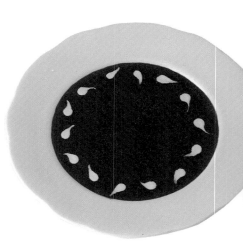

1 Flood a plate with dark, coloured sauce. Fill a piping (pastry) bag fitted with a small nozzle (tube) with cream. Pipe dots of cream evenly spaced around the edge of the bowl.

2 Use the point of a fine metal skewer to drag the cream through the sauce to form a 'tail'.

An Ice Bowl

Use the ice bowl when serving ice cream and sorbets. To make, you will need two freezerproof mixing bowls, one much smaller than the other. The smaller bowl should be plastic.

1 Boil sufficient water to fill the larger bowl and leave it to cool. Place the larger bowl in the kitchen sink and pour in the cool boiled water. Float the plastic bowl inside the larger bowl and weigh it down so that it is partly submerged. Use freezer tape to keep it in place. Place both bowls in the freezer.

2 When the water between the bowls begins to freeze, push rose petals and other edible flowers and herb leaves down between the two bowls. Use a metal skewer to do this. Do not try to push too many flowers or leaves down at once or the decoration will be all bunched together and the result will be less attractive.

3 When the water has frozen, remove the bowls. Dip the bottom bowl in hot water and twist off. Quickly fill the top bowl with hot water, pour it out again and twist off.

Frosting Fruit and Flowers

Use these to decorate cakes and desserts. Remember to use only edible flowers. Gum arabic is available from specialist cake decorating supply shops.

Brush the outside of soft fruit, such as grapes, strawberries, raspberries and blackberries with a little lightly beaten egg white, then sift with caster (superfine) sugar or roll them in the sugar. Use the same technique for frosting flowers. If preferred, for a crisper finish, the flowers can be brushed with gum arabic mixed with water instead of egg white.

Frosted Fruit and Flower

Chocolate Caraque

Use to decorate desserts or cakes. Chill if not using straightaway.

Melt plain (semi-sweet), white or dark chocolate in a bowl placed over a saucepan of hot water. Spread the melted chocolate on a sheet of greaseproof paper (waxed paper) or a slab of marble in an even, thin layer. Leave until just set. Using a sharp kitchen knife held at an acute angle, shave off long curls of chocolate.

Chocolate Shapes

Use to decorate cakes. Again, they can be placed on the cake at once, or stored in the refrigerator until required.

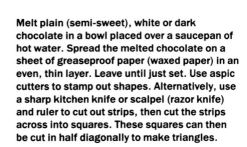

Melt plain (semi-sweet), white or dark chocolate in a bowl placed over a saucepan of hot water. Spread the melted chocolate on a sheet of greaseproof paper (waxed paper) in an even, thin layer. Leave until just set. Use aspic cutters to stamp out shapes. Alternatively, use a sharp kitchen knife or scalpel (razor knife) and ruler to cut out strips, then cut the strips across into squares. These squares can then be cut in half diagonally to make triangles.

Chocolate Rose Leaves

Choose any non-poisonous leaves, such as rose leaves, to make this attractive decoration for cakes and desserts.

Melt plain (semi-sweet), white or dark chocolate in a bowl placed over a saucepan of hot water. Using a small brush, brush a thin layer of melted chocolate on the underside of each leaf. When the chocolate has dried, it will easily separate from the leaf.

Marzipan Fruits.

Marzipan Fruits
Use bought white marzipan (almond paste) and colour it using paste food colours (food colouring). Mould small balls of paste of the appropriate colour into miniature fruits. Finish oranges by rolling them on a nutmeg grater to achieve the correct texture and add the end of a clove for a stalk (stem); paint bananas with brown food colouring; use pale green paste for pears and dust them with red powder food colouring; use cloves for stalks on apples or on a bunch of grapes. Arrange the fruit in paper cases (cups) and serve them as petits fours or small gifts.

Stuffed Dates
Stuff fresh dates with marzipan (almond paste) and roll in caster (superfine) sugar. Candied dates may also be stuffed and included among a box of chocolates.

Toasted Nuts
Toasted flaked almonds, chopped hazelnuts and desiccated (shredded) coconut are ideal to sprinkle over desserts and for pressing on the side of cakes. Lay the nuts on a foil-lined grill (broiler) pan and toast well away from the heat, turning the nuts often so they brown evenly and do not burn.

Crushed Crumbs
Place plain biscuits (cookies) in a clean plastic bag and crush them with a rolling pin. Crushed crumbs are delicious sprinkled over soft desserts to add a little crunch or use them as coating for cakes covered in a buttercream or soft icing.

Strawberry Fans
Part-slice strawberries, cutting thin slices and leaving them attached at the stalk (stem) end. Gently ease the slices apart sideways. This fanning technique may be used for savoury ingredients such as baby carrots, small cucumbers and gherkins (pickles).

BREAKFASTS AND BRUNCHES

and cheery, a better option for brunch. Guests can be invited any time from 10 a.m. to 11.30 a.m. at the latest for a brunch party.

A breakfast party can be a good way of getting a special day off to a social start. You may invite friends for a casual breakfast before setting off for a day trip into the country, or before the local carnival, town parade or other similar festive event. Linking breakfast in this way means that you can allow guests to lounge around without having to indulge in deep conversation because everyone will have plenty of opportunity to chat later. Allow a couple of hours before everyone has to leave the house.

*E*ntertaining first thing in the day is not everyone's style and many people prefer not to be sociable before lunch, so breakfasts should not be formal, early morning affairs. Decide whether you want your party to be extremely lazy and relaxed – a good idea for breakfast gatherings – or bright

LAZY BREAKFAST

Make this party easy on yourself as well as the guests. Keep the cooking to a minimum by preparing a large continental-style breakfast platter. Make croissants in advance and have them warming in the oven. Warm bagels and serve them with bowls of cream cheese and smoked salmon (lox). Include doughnuts or Danish pastries for those who enjoy sweet treats and have an enormous basket of fruit as a centrepiece so that everyone can help themselves. Keep the coffee and tea brewing all the time.

❖ Arrange a large flat basket full of unusual teas as alternative drinks – fruit tea sachets, bundles of herb teas and

sprigs of rosemary, lemon balm and different types of mint. Place small glass dishes of thinly sliced lemon, orange and lime around the basket, with tongs for guests to serve themselves. Remember to set out a bowl of sugar lumps, too.

❖ Make sure you are well stocked with different fruit juices and prepare a jug of an early morning awakener:

orange, lemon and lime slices, thin cucumber slices, mint sprigs, rosemary sprigs and several good dashes of bitters. Top up with sparkling mineral water (seltzer). Serve this on its own or use it as a mixer for topping up glasses of chilled sparkling wine.

Breakfast and Brunch Checklist

- Cereal
- Fruit
- Savoury dishes
- Milk
- Sugar
- Coffee
- Tea
- Sparkling wines
- Fruit juices
- Any special dietary needs?
- Table linen
- Cutlery (flatware), china and glassware
- Flowers
- House cleaning and tidying

A cooling glass of mint tea.

Table Style for Brunch

Select sunny colours – yellows, oranges and greens.

❖ Arrange bowls of fresh, fragrant herbs around the room.

❖ Make lots of pomanders using oranges and lemons. Stud the fruit all over with cloves, then pile them high in colourful pottery bowls and distribute them around the house.

❖ Decorate a plain cloth with ribbon flowers, arranging them in groups of three on the corners or around the edge of the cloth. Sew on silk leaves, tucking them under the flowers. Make ribbon rosebuds and stitch small groups of them at intervals around the cloth, between the larger flowers.

BRIGHT BRUNCH IDEAS

As a complete contrast to the laid-back breakfast, opt for a livelier feeling when entertaining mid-morning. Move the party out into the garden on summer mornings or have all the windows open and tie back curtains with bows of spring-coloured ribbons.

❖ Serve two or more courses or lay out a buffet for larger gatherings. Greet guests with Buck's Fizz (Mimosa, a mixture of sparkling wine and orange juice), wine spritzers or kir (sparkling wine flavoured with cassis) .

❖ Make simple fruit salads and cocktails and have bowls of yogurt to serve with them.

❖ Serve pitted, ready-to-eat prunes wrapped in bacon and grilled as a hot starter (appetizer).

❖ Have a kitchen brunch and cook waffles, blinis or pancakes as they are needed. If you have the batter all mixed and ready to cook, then encourage guests to fix their own. Make sure you have at least a couple of pans or electric waffle irons ready to heat. Alternatively, make stacks in advance and let your guests heat their own.

❖ Organize a seafood brunch: serve smoked salmon, prawns (shrimp) marinated with herbs and lemon, grilled oysters, smoked mackerel and scallop kebabs (scallop kebabs are delicious wrapped in a piece of bacon, for example). Serve dressed crab, grilled lobster and poached salmon for an extra special brunch occasion.

Take a Scottish theme, and use tartan cloth for the table and serve a bowl of hot porridge (oatmeal).

79

BREAKFAST FRUIT COCKTAIL

———— SERVES 4 ————

This zesty fruit cocktail is the perfect first
course for a sit-down brunch party or it is ideal
for a breakfast buffet table.

1 mango
2 pink or yellow grapefruit
3 oranges
1 charentais or cantaloupe melon
mint sprigs to decorate

TO SERVE
Greek yogurt or fromage frais
runny honey

1 Peel the mango, then slice the fruit off the
stone (pit) and cut it into bite-sized pieces.
Prepare the grapefruit and oranges: slice off
the peel and pith from the top and bottom of
each fruit, then use a sharp serrated knife to
cut the rind and pith off the sides in wide strips,
working all around the fruit.

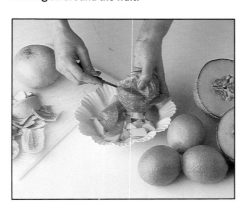

2 Once all the peel and pith is removed, slice
the grapefruit and oranges, and cut the slices
in half. Halve the melon, discard the seeds,
then cut the halves into quarters. Cut the flesh
into strips with a knife, then across into pieces
(still attached to the skin). Cut between the
skin and the melon flesh to form neat pieces.

3 Mix all the fruit and add the mint sprigs.
Cover and chill for at least 30 minutes,
preferably a couple of hours. Pick out the mint
sprigs and arrange them on top of the fruit
before serving. Offer the yogurt or fromage
frais and honey separately.

Breakfast Fruit Cocktail.

SEEDED CROISSANTS

———— MAKES 8 ————

Home-made croissants really are worth the
effort, especially as they can be made in a
large batch and frozen before or after baking.
This recipe is slightly different from traditional
croissant recipes, having a small proportion of
wholemeal (whole-wheat) flour and a crunchy
topping of poppy seeds or sesame seeds.

350 g/12 oz (3 cups) strong plain (bread) flour
100 g/4 oz (1 cup) wholemeal (whole-wheat)
flour
1 teaspoon salt
1 teaspoon caster (superfine) sugar
400 g/14 oz (1¾ cups) butter
1 sachet (envelope) easy-blend (quick-rising)
dried yeast
250 ml/8 fl oz (1 cup) lukewarm water
1 egg, beaten
poppy seeds or sesame seeds for topping

1 Mix together both types of flour, the salt and
sugar in a bowl. Rub in (cut in) 50 g/2 oz
(¼ cup) of the butter. Divide the remaining
butter into 3 equal portions and shape each
into a 10 cm/4 in square. Chill. Stir the yeast
into the flour mixture .

2 Bind the flour mixture with the water to make a firm dough.

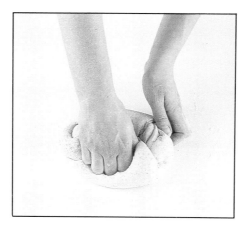

3 Turn out the dough onto a floured surface and knead well for about 10 minutes, or until it feels very smooth and elastic. The dough is kneaded sufficiently when it springs back quickly if pressed with a fingertip.

4 Roll out the dough into an oblong shape measuring about 30 × 12.5 cm/12 × 5 in. Place a square of chilled butter in the middle of the dough, then fold the bottom third portion of the dough up over the butter.

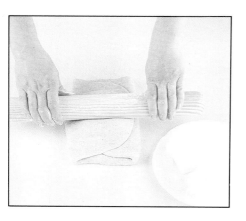

5 Fold the top third of the dough down, then seal the edges by pressing them with a rolling pin. Chill the dough for 5 minutes.

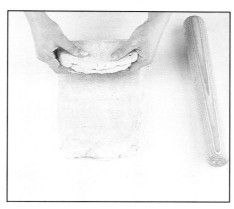

6 Roll out and fold the dough a further 2 times the same way to incorporate the remaining butter, chilling between each rolling. Then repeat the process again without any butter so the dough has been rolled and folded 6 times in all. Chill the dough well at the end of rolling.

7 Grease 2 baking sheets. Cut the dough in half. Roll out one portion into a 30 cm/12 in square and cut it diagonally into quarters, then cut into 8 triangles.

8 Roll up each triangle of dough from the long side towards the point. Place on a baking sheet and curve the rolled portions of dough to shape the croissants. Repeat with the remaining dough. Cover the dough loosely with oiled plastic or place in a large plastic bag and leave to rise in a cool room for several hours. Alternatively, leave the croissants in the refrigerator to rise overnight. If the croissants are placed in a warm room, the butter will melt and they will become greasy and poorly risen.

9 Set the oven at 220°C/425°F/Gas 7. Brush the tops of the croissants very gently with beaten egg and sprinkle generously with poppy seeds or sesame seeds. Bake for 15–20 minutes, until the croissants are risen and golden. Cool on a wire rack.

Seeded Croissant.

FREEZE AHEAD

To freeze the croissants before baking, allow them to rise completely, then open freeze them on their baking sheets and pack them in freezerproof bags when they are firm.

To freeze the baked croissants, leave them to cool completely before sealing in a plastic bag. Either way, the croissants benefit from being stored in a rigid container to prevent damage. Bake raw croissants from frozen, allowing about 5 minutes extra baking time.

Wheat Basket

Bring new life to an old or drab wire basket by trimming it with wheat and toning buff-coloured paper ribbon. Wire containers intended for kitchen use look good decorated this way.

YOU WILL NEED: wire basket, twisted buff-coloured paper, dried wheat and other grass heads, dried poppy seed heads, raffia, scissors.

1 Thread a length of twisted, buff-coloured paper at intervals through the loops around the basket edge. Open out some of the paper once it is in position.

2 Tie the ends of the paper in an attractive knot or bow. Tie small bundles of wheat and grass heads together with raffia, including a poppy seed head in some of the bundles.

3 Position the bundles of grasses around the edges of the basket, between the opened-out sections of paper. Bind in place with raffia, tying neat knots and trimming the ends.

EUROPEAN BREAKFAST PLATTER

—————— SERVES 4 (see Cook's Tip) ——————

A platter of cold food looks great on a brunch buffet. It is also excellent for a sit-down breakfast with overnight guests, as it is simple to prepare and especially easy to serve, allowing you to relax and late-risers to share the meal without any last-minute cooking and embarrassing fuss. Of course, you do not have to follow rigidly the combination of ingredients used here — vary the selection of cold meats and fruit according to taste, but ensure that the display is colourful, neat and attractive. Ideally, poach the apricots the night before to allow them plenty of time to cool down and absorb flavour.

225 g/8 oz (1⅓ cups) ready-to-eat
dried apricots
100 ml/4 fl oz (½ cup) unsweetened
apple juice
2 tablespoons cider vinegar
2 cloves
1 cinnamon stick, 7.5 cm/3 in
4 eggs, hard-boiled, shelled and quartered
1 tablespoon chopped fresh dill
2 tablespoons soured cream
about 1 tablespoon milk
salt and freshly ground black pepper
4 ripe tomatoes, sliced
8 slices mortadella
4 slices cooked ham
12 slices salami
225 g/8 oz Gruyère or Emmenthal (Swiss)
cheese, thinly sliced
100 g/4 oz feta cheese, cubed
100 g/4 oz Edam or Gouda cheese, cubed
50 g/2 oz (⅓ cup) black (ripe) olives,
stoned (pitted)
8 cocktail gherkins (pickles)
sprigs of dill, to garnish (optional)

European Breakfast Platter.

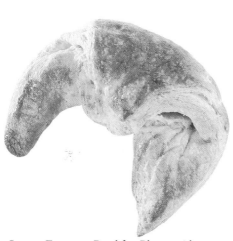

Serve a European Breakfast Platter with a range of breakfast breads, such as croissants, seeded rolls and French-style baguettes.

Place the apricots in a small saucepan. Add the apple juice, cider vinegar, cloves and cinnamon stick. Heat gently until the liquid boils, cover the pan and simmer for 7—10 minutes, until most of the liquid is absorbed. Leave to stand until completely cold.

Arrange the eggs at one end of a large serving platter. Mix together the dill and soured cream. Stir in just enough milk to give a thick pouring consistency. Add a little seasoning, then trickle this dressing over the eggs. Arrange the tomatoes, cold meats and cheeses on the platter, then add the olives and gherkins (pickles) as appropriate. Garnish with sprigs of dill, if liked.

Keep or discard the spices from the apricots, as liked. They can be served in a separate bowl or add them to the platter to separate the meats from the cheeses.

COOK'S TIP
The quantities given apply when the platter is served as the main dish for a sit-down breakfast; the amounts do not have to be multiplied in proportion when preparing a buffet for a larger gathering as guests will eat less from the platter.

LUNCHEON OPTIONS

*T*he majority of lunchtime entertaining is concentrated into weekends and holidays, and what better opportunity for meeting friends and families, forgetting about formalities and relaxing with simple food in good company. Keep the menu unfussy and plan to meet friends for some

form of activity in the morning, perhaps a shopping session, or to participate in a favourite sport, or organize a swim at the local pool with adults and children.

Larger gatherings can be successful too – make sure you provide for young guests as well as adults and take advantage of fine weather to keep children happy outdoors. If you invite several families with children of roughly the same ages, then you will not have to bother about organizing games. As soon as introductions are over, shyness fades fast and children quickly establish common interests using their imagination to create their own entertainment. As long as it's not disruptive, let it happen and concentrate on the adults.

INVITATIONS

Formal lunches are fixed for 1 p.m. and you may want to invite guests half an hour earlier so that you can offer them an aperitif. Cards do not have to be sent to a small group, simply ring around one or two weeks in advance to reserve the day.

LUNCH MENUS

Two courses are adequate for any lunch, perhaps together with a cheese board. Unless you are serving a roast Sunday lunch, the menu should be light and fairly delicate. A light soup and some grilled fish or poultry with seasonal vegetables or salad are suitable. A vegetable terrine with salad and new potatoes or quiche lorraine with salad are all typical dishes.

HEARTY WEEKEND LUNCHES Quite different from delicate social affairs, these are for action-packed weekends when everyone is planning to get out in the fresh air and expend some energy before lunch or later in the afternoon. Chunky soups, warm breads, hearty pasta and rice dishes and full-flavoured pâtés all fit the bill.

SUNDAY LUNCH This is not a snatched meal – especially if serving up a roast – and plenty of time should be set aside to linger over the dessert, cheese (if serving) and coffee. Three courses may be served, or offer a light dip and crudités with drinks beforehand instead of a first course.

A rib of beef or standing rib roast has to be the ultimate joint for such occasions. Cooked to perfection, served with rich gravy, mashed or golden roast potatoes, creamy mashed parsnips, glazed carrots or crunchy steamed Brussels sprouts, this is what traditional Sunday lunch is all about!

For dessert consider apple pie and custard (custard sauce) or ice cream; creamy baked rice pudding served with a compote of plums or smooth orange syllabub.

To cook a roast to perfection, it is important to have everything well planned in advance: peel potatoes and prepare vegetables and keep them covered with water (not a good idea for everyday cooking as you lose precious vitamins but practical on occasion), cook and mash parsnips ready to reheat and have the dessert prepared.

Lunch Checklist

- Nibbles (snacks)
- First course
- Main course
- Dessert
- Wine and/or beer
- Alcohol-free drinks
- Ice
- Coffee
- Any special dietary needs?
- Table linen
- Cutlery (flatware), china and glassware
- Flowers
- House cleaning and tidying

LITTLE EMPANADAS

——— MAKES 24 ———

These tiny empanadas, or turnovers, are ideal for handing around with drinks. They also look attractive arranged on individual plates, with a small garnish of salad; however, for a less elegant result simply shape the dough into 12 small turnovers.

450 g/1 lb (4 cups) strong white (bread) flour
1 sachet (envelope) easy-blend (quick-rising) dried yeast
1 teaspoon salt
1 teaspoon caster (superfine) sugar
275 ml/9 fl oz (1 cup plus 2 tablespoons) lukewarm water

FILLING
2 tablespoons olive oil
1 onion, finely chopped
1 garlic clove, crushed
1 small green pepper (sweet bell pepper), seeded and finely diced
1 small red pepper (sweet bell pepper), seeded and finely diced
450 g/1 lb boneless chicken breast, skinned and finely diced
2 tablespoons black (ripe) olives, stoned (pitted) and chopped
salt and freshly ground black pepper
1 teaspoon dried oregano
2 teaspoons ground coriander
¼ teaspoon chilli powder
3 tablespoons raisins (optional)
1 egg, beaten, to glaze

Gazpacho.

Prepare the filling first: heat the oil in a saucepan. Add the onion, garlic, green and red peppers, and cook, stirring occasionally, for 5 minutes. Stir in the chicken and continue to cook until the chicken pieces are firm and lightly cooked. Stir in the olives, seasoning, oregano, coriander, chilli powder and raisins (if used), then cook for 2 minutes. Remove the pan from the heat and set aside.

Grease 2 baking sheets. Mix together the flour, yeast, salt, sugar and water to make a firm dough. Turn out the dough on to a lightly floured surface and knead it thoroughly for about 10 minutes, until it is smooth and elastic. Divide the dough in half. Keep one half covered with plastic while you work with the other, first cutting it into 12 equal pieces.

Flatten a small piece of dough into a circle measuring about 8.5 cm/3½ in across. Place a little of the chicken mixture in the middle of the dough and dampen the edge, then fold the dough in half to enclose the filling completely in a semi-circular pasty. Pinch the edges to seal in the filling. Continue shaping the pasties, placing them on the baking sheets as they are filled. Cover with oiled cling film (plastic wrap) and leave in a warm place until the dough is risen. Meanwhile, set the oven at 220°C/425°F/Gas 7.

Brush the empanadas with beaten egg and bake them for 15–20 minutes, until golden brown. Transfer to a wire rack to cool.

GAZPACHO

——— SERVES 6 ———

This Spanish soup, flavoured with garlic and vegetables and thickened with breadcrumbs, is usually served chilled. It is perfect for a summer lunch on the patio, and the quantities can easily be multiplied for a large party.

75 g/3 oz (1½ cups) fresh breadcrumbs
100 ml/4 fl oz (½ cup) water
2 tablespoons cider vinegar
250 ml/8 fl oz (1 cup) tomato juice
1 onion, chopped
1 cucumber, peeled and roughly chopped
2 garlic cloves, crushed
1 kg/2 lb ripe tomatoes, peeled and seeded
1 red pepper (sweet bell pepper), seeded and roughly chopped
2 teaspoons caster (superfine) sugar
6 tablespoons olive oil
salt and freshly ground black pepper
cayenne pepper

GARNISH
croûtons
black (ripe) olives, stoned (pitted) and sliced
1 green pepper (sweet bell pepper), seeded and diced
1 onion, chopped

Place the breadcrumbs in a bowl. Sprinkle the water, cider vinegar and tomato juice over and leave to soak for 15 minutes.

Using a food processor or blender, purée the onion, cucumber, garlic, tomatoes and red pepper until they are smooth. Add the sugar and process the mixture again, then slowly work in the olive oil. Add the soaked breadcrumbs with all the juice and blend until smooth.

Add seasoning and a little cayenne pepper, then taste the gazpacho to check the seasoning. Chill well before serving.

Offer the croûtons, olives, green pepper and onion in separate bowls so that they may be sprinkled over individual portions as required.

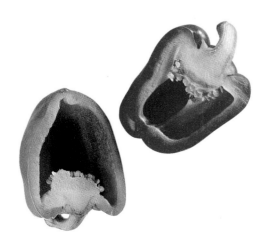

OPEN SANDWICHES

Open sandwiches are impressive and appetizing for lunch parties of all sizes. They do need a fair amount of last-minute attention, however, if they are going to look and, more importantly, taste their best. If you want to prepare open sandwiches for more than eight people, to avoid being over-burdened with last-minute garnishes keep the menu simple, serving only the sandwiches and a prepared-ahead dessert.

Trying to set out a stunning array of sandwiches is hopeless if you do not have suitable platters on which to present them. Large meat platters will do but the sandwiches look awkward on wide rims of deep platters. Use large flat cake stands, cheese boards and glass or marble platters.

If you are stuck for serving dishes, buy metal or plastic trays and dress them up by wiring herb sprigs together and taping them around the tray's rim on the outside. Cover the middle of the tray with plain paper doilies or paper napkins to match your table style.

The following is a guide to bases, flavoured butters, spreads and toppings with notes on what to prepare several hours in advance and the essential last-minute additions.

Bases

WHITE BREAD Select an unsliced, square-shaped, sandwich loaf. Cut the crusts off the outside before slicing. This should be sliced fairly thickly and the slices can be cut diagonally to make triangular sandwiches. White bread is good for light seafood toppings and chicken or turkey mixtures.

LIGHT RYE BREAD Close-textured light rye bread makes a versatile and firm base for all sorts of toppings, including delicate ingredients such as smoked salmon and caviar-style fish roe. It is not necessary to cut the crusts off.

DARK OR BLACK RYE BREAD This tends to have a moister texture than light rye, so it breaks more easily. However, it is more sturdy than ordinary white or wholemeal (whole-wheat) bread, so it can be sliced fairly thinly. The flavour is quite strong and slightly tangy, and the bread usually includes caraway or fennel seeds. Some people like this with smoked salmon, while others prefer the milder light rye. Rye bread is excellent with strong smoked fish, such as mackerel or trout.

PUMPERNICKEL Moist, close-textured, tangy and distinctly flavoured, pumpernickel is another candidate for serving with smoked fish and soured cream (fresh sour cream). Herrings are a good topping with chopped dill and sliced raw onion. Full-flavoured meats, such as pastrami and garlic sausages, also go well on pumpernickel.

ROLLS, CROISSANTS AND BAGELS Split horizontally, these all make suitable bases but they can look messy if you are not careful and there is more filling than sliced bread. Plain ingredients are the best toppings for rich croissants – smoked ham, finely sliced Emmenthal (Swiss) or Gruyère cheese, thinly sliced smoked turkey – while mixed ingredients with more dominant flavours go well with rolls and bagels. Spicy meats, such as pastrami, mortadella, salami and frankfurters and mixed creamy-dressed salads are also good on thicker bases.

FRENCH BREAD This is fine for *al fresco* eating, where delicacy does not feature on the menu! Cut a slim baguette into pieces, then slice them in half lengthways. Use chunky toppings which stay in place well, such as mayonnaise-dressed prawns (shrimp), chicken or rolled ham.

WHOLE-GRAIN BREAD Loaves with added whole grains make a pleasing texture for substantial toppings. Avoid the plain, very light wholemeal (whole-wheat) loaves which tend to be slightly dry and uninteresting. Some of the pre-sliced multi-grain loaves make good bases. Halve slices from large loaves with a rounded shape.

Butters and Spreads

Soften butter before spreading so it does not tear the bread base. Unsalted, lightly salted or salted butter may be used according to taste; consider the delicate flavour of foods such as smoked trout fillets or Parma ham (prosciutto) and you may decide to opt for unsalted butter even if you do not usually use it.

Flavoured butters should be chosen to complement the topping. Here are a few suggestions.

PARSLEY BUTTER Chopped fresh parsley adds a refreshing flavour to butter for the majority of toppings, but its flavour is wasted with highly seasoned ingredients, such as curried chicken.

LEMON BUTTER Finely grated lemon rind (peel) adds a distinct flavour which is good with fish and seafood, chicken and turkey.

MIXED HERB BUTTER Chopped fresh parsley, thyme, basil, tarragon, a hint of sage and rosemary and a little mint combine well. A mixed herb butter is ideal for vegetable-based toppings, such as lettuce and tomatoes, and for yeast pâtés, eggs or cheese.

A selection of tasty open sandwiches: top tray, Italian Ham with Mango; bottom tray, left, Smoked Mackerel, and right, Smoked Salmon with Dill.

ANCHOVY BUTTER Flavour unsalted butter with anchovy essence (extract) or create a stronger spread by pounding canned anchovies and their oil to a paste before beating into butter. Add a dash of lemon juice and some freshly ground black pepper. Use as a base for roast beef, eggs or salad ingredients, such as cucumbers and tomatoes.

Toppings

The topping should centre on one or two main ingredients, possibly with a lettuce or tomato base and with a complementary garnish. Unusual cheeses or vegetable pâtés are tasty choices for vegetarians. You can serve almost anything on an open sandwich, so the following are intended only as suggestions to fire your imagination.

SMOKED SALMON WITH DILL This is a classic open sandwich topping for lunch, breakfast or brunch. Fold and overlap thin slices of smoked salmon on light rye bread. Parsley butter may be spread on the bread, if liked. Garnish just before serving, with small dollops of soured cream (fresh sour cream) and a sprinkling of fresh dill, and add a small wedge of lemon. The juice from the lemon is squeezed over the sandwich. A dill sprig may be added for an extra garnish.

SMOKED MACKEREL Spread horseradish sauce or creamed horseradish over the base. Top with flaked smoked mackerel or other smoked fish if preferred. Cover at this stage with cling film (plastic wrap) and set aside until ready to serve. Add a garnish of diced, peeled and seeded tomato, diced fresh or dill cucumber and very finely chopped onion or flat leaf parsley just before serving.

ITALIAN HAM WITH MANGO Trim the fat from Parma ham (prosciutto) and arrange it in folds on a base of white bread. Cover with cling film (plastic wrap) at this stage and set aside, ready for last minute garnishing. When ready to serve, add a little radicchio or chicory (endive), a couple of slices of fresh mango and a few shreds of fresh basil. Garnish with basil sprigs at the last minute and trickle a little olive oil over the ham, if liked.

BACON, LETTUCE AND TOMATO Spread the bread with anchovy butter, soft cheese flavoured with garlic and herbs or mixed herb butter. Add the rest of the topping no longer than 30 minutes before serving. Top with lettuce leaves and coleslaw or grated carrot. Add some mayonnaise or soured cream (fresh sour cream) and sprinkle with crisp bacon. Garnish with cherry tomatoes, if liked.

AVOCADO AND PESTO This is a sandwich to assemble at the last minute. Arrange lettuce leaves on the bread base and top them with sliced avocado. Trickle a little pesto over the avocado and serve.

Felt Flower Napkin Rings

Choose fine, smooth felt and ribbon in colours to match or harmonize with your table settings.

YOU WILL NEED: (for each napkin ring) thin card (posterboard) for template, pencil, scissors, coloured and green felt, needle and thread to match, a few tiny beads; (for each felt flower) 90 cm/1 yd velvet ribbon about 1.5 cm/⅝ in wide, needle and thread to match, 20 cm/8 in plastic-covered tying wire, wire cutters.

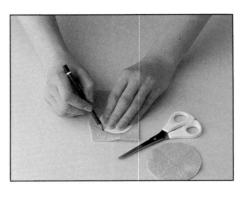

1 Cut out two circular templates, one 6.5 cm/2½ in in diameter and the other 4 cm/1½ in. Draw the outlines onto the felt and cut out.

2 Fold each felt circle in quarters and cut a shallow V-shape out of the curved edge to make scalloped 'petals'.

3 Sew a tiny ring of running stitches around the centre of each flower shape, then pull the thread to pucker the centre slightly.

4 Stitch the smaller circle on top of the larger one. Sew three or four beads in the centre.

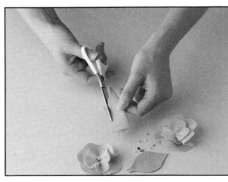

5 Cut out two leaf shapes from green felt.

6 Place the leaves on the underside of the flower and stitch.

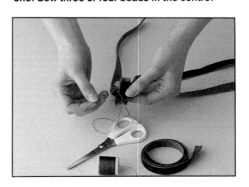

7 Cut the ribbon into three equal lengths. Stitch the ribbon lengths together at one end with matching thread.

8 Plait (braid) the ribbon neatly and not too tightly so that it forms an even band.

9 Secure the end of the plait with a few stitches and trim.

10 Run a length of plastic-covered tying wire along the back of the plait, securing it in place with a few stitches here and there.

11 Form the plait into a ring, twisting the ends of the wire together to secure. Trim off the excess wire with wire cutters. Turn the ends of the plait under and stitch together.

12 Sew the flower to the plait to cover the join.

continued . . .

continued . . .

A red poppy napkin ring will bring a splash of colour to a summer lunch table. The plaited (braided) ring is made in the same way as before.

YOU WILL NEED: (for each poppy) thin card (posterboard) for template, pencil, scissors, red felt, needle and thread to match, black haberdashers' wire for stamens; (for each napkin ring) 90 cm/1 yd velvet ribbon, 20 cm/8 in plastic-covered tying wire, wire cutters.

13 Make a card template for a three-lobed poppy shape about 7.5 cm/3 in in diameter. Draw the outline onto the felt.

14 Cut out two poppy shapes for each flower.

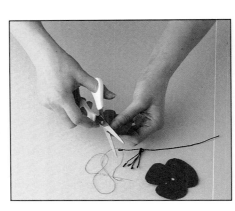

15 Fold the flower to find the centre and cut a tiny nick with scissors.

16 Lay the two poppy shapes together with the lobes at different angles. Shape hooked stamens using haberdashers' wire.

17 Insert the stamens into the centre of the poppy from front to back. Twist the wire around the base of the flower once or twice.

18 Stitch the wire to the base of the poppy to secure. Attach the poppy to the plaited napkin ring as before (see step 12).

INVITATION TO TEA

*T*ea usually falls into two categories, either an elegant social event taken on the lawn in summer or a heart-warming meeting for fresh toasted buns, lots of steaming hot tea and tall sundaes.

Long gone are the days when taking tea meant sitting on best behaviour, making stilted conversation and nibbling the tiniest of sandwiches. Even the most sophisticated events should be relaxed and pleasant, with guests free to move about and catch up with old friends.

SENDING OUT INVITATIONS

Depending on the size and type of gathering, invitations may be informal and made by telephone a week or two ahead or they may be written and sent three or four weeks before the event.

Informal invitations imply a homely menu and simple entertainment, perhaps a game of charades or cards. Guests will usually come in smart, casual clothes and this may be an opportunity to meet new members of the family.

Written invitations suggest a grander event. It is up to you to decide whether you want everyone to make a special effort to dress up. For example you may opt for a tea party in the garden and ask all the women to wear hats. One way of making the message unmistakably clear is to cut out novelty invitations in the shape of hats and to dress them up with ribbon, feathers, flowers and bows.

TABLE DRESSINGS

Lace cloths and fine decorative linens are *de rigueur* for a formal tea party. If there is a buffet arrangement for food, a plain white cloth covered by a lace overcloth looks pretty. Tie the lace cloth in swags and decorate it with posies of roses and ribbon bows.

❖ Tie linen napkins with lace and carefully place a rosebud or a small flower in each. Make a pretty bow by covering a length of satin ribbon with very fine lace. Ribbon of a delicate colour may be used to match a coloured undercloth on the table.

❖ Wire small roses or rosebuds, then trim the stems and wrap them with florists' tape. A small safety pin stuck discreetly through the back of the tape enables the flowers to be worn as buttonholes or they can be pinned to hats.

❖ For a sit-down tea, decorate the table with tulle bonbonnières, or sweet (candy) cups, for each place setting.

Planning for Large Tea Parties

❖ Some cakes may be made and frozen well ahead.

❖ Sweet pastry cases (pie crusts) can be prepared and cooked for strawberry tarts, then frozen unfilled. Thaw, then warm the cases in the oven briefly before adding a fresh-fruit filling.

❖ Sandwiches should be made on the day of the party; however, fillings that require mixing, such as egg mayonnaise, can be prepared the day before and kept covered in the refrigerator.

❖ Ice cream for sundaes should be scooped out onto baking trays or

into large, shallow containers lined with cling film (plastic wrap) early in the day, then covered and frozen. Glasses for sundaes should be placed on their sides in the refrigerator a few hours ahead if space allows. This makes the process of assembling sundaes quick and easy.

❖ Lay out cups and saucers on a trolley or several trays. Remember to put teaspoons on the saucers. Have small plates and napkins ready.

❖ Have several large teapots ready. If you are entertaining a large crowd, hire (rent) a tea urn from a caterers' or party supply store.

Bonbonnières

These charming lacy holders for candies or sweets are easy to make and look pretty strewn about the table.

YOU WILL NEED: for each holder a circle of tulle or lace about 15 cm/6 in in diameter plus trimming, needle and thread, ribbons, sugared almonds, pastel-coloured mints, cashews, mixed nuts or other confectionery.

1 Hem the edge of the fabric circle and trim it with lace, if you like.

2 Place a few sugared almonds or other confectionery in the centre of the circle of fabric. Tie up the bonbonnière into a neat bundle with fine satin ribbon. Attach a small name tag if you like and place the bonbonnières in position on the table.

Minted Cucumber Sandwiches

Beat a tablespoon of chopped fresh mint into 100 g/4 oz (½ cup) butter. Peel and thinly slice half a cucumber. Spread out the cucumber slices on a dish and sprinkle them with a little salt, then set aside for 20 minutes. Pat dry the cucumber slices with absorbent kitchen paper (paper towels). Season with a little freshly ground black pepper. Spread 16 thin slices of white bread thinly with the minted butter. Arrange a layer of cucumber slices and top with thin slices of white bread. Trim off the crusts and cut into neat triangles. Makes 64.

DELICATE SANDWICHES

Sandwiches served with afternoon tea should be slim, delicately flavoured and very elegant.

❖ Use bread that is one day old but make sure it is not stale.

❖ Butter must be softened so it spreads easily and thinly.

❖ Fillings should be finely cut or prepared so they form a thin, even layer; at the same time, the flavour of the filling must come through well.

❖ Always cut off the crusts – use a sharp serrated knife and trim each sandwich individually.

❖ Cut the sandwiches diagonally into quarters to make small, neat triangles.

❖ Arrange sandwiches on plates and cover with cling film (plastic wrap), then keep cool until required.

Watercress Rolls

These add variety to your sandwich platter. Trim and chop a bunch of watercress, then beat it with 100 g/4 oz (½ cup) cream cheese. Add seasoning and a little grated nutmeg to taste. If necessary, stir in a little milk to soften the cheese mixture so it spreads easily. Cut the crusts off 8 slices of white bread. Roll the bread lightly with a rolling pin so it is quite thin. Spread with the watercress mixture, then roll up each slice from the short side. Wrap each roll in cling film (plastic wrap). Use a serrated knife to slice each roll in half before serving. Makes 16.

Make the most of a leisurely afternoon tea, with piles of freshly made sandwiches and a range of delicious home-made cakes.

TRADITIONAL SCONES

—————— MAKES 20 ——————

Served with clotted cream and jam, these traditional scones epitomize the country-style afternoon tea.

450 g/1lb (4 cups) plain (all-purpose) flour
4 teaspoons cream of tartar
2 teaspoons bicarbonate of soda (baking soda)
½ teaspoon salt
100 g/4 oz (½ cup) butter
50 g/2 oz (¼ cup) caster (superfine) sugar
about 250 ml/8 fl oz (1 cup) milk
extra milk to glaze

Serve scones with jam and cream.

Set the oven at 230°C/450°F/Gas 8. Grease 2 baking sheets. Sift the flour, cream of tartar, bicarbonate of soda (baking soda) and salt into a bowl. Rub in (cut in) the butter until it is finely blended with the flour. Stir in the caster (superfine) sugar and add the milk. Mix the dough to a soft but not too sticky consistency, adding a little extra milk if necessary.

Turn out the dough onto a lightly floured surface and roll it out to about 1 cm/½ in thick. Use a fluted cutter to stamp out 20 rounds of dough, lightly re-rolling the trimmings if necessary, but do not over-work the dough. Place them on the prepared baking sheets. Brush the scones with a little milk. Bake for 7–10 minutes, until well risen and lightly browned. Cool the scones on a wire rack.

PREPARE AHEAD
Scones freeze extremely well and they thaw quickly in a hot oven. They are good for breakfast, with butter and jam or marmalade, as well as for afternoon tea.

Dried Fruit Kuchen.

DRIED FRUIT KUCHEN

—————— MAKES 16 PIECES ——————

This is a delicious and unusual yeast-based cake, very much in the style of Eastern-European baking.

175 g/6 oz (1 cup) ready-to-eat dried apricots
175 g/6 oz (1 cup) ready-to-eat dried peaches
100 g/4 oz (²/₃ cup) ready-to-eat dried apple rings
300 ml/½ pint (1¼ cups) orange juice
350 g/12 oz (3 cups) strong plain (bread) flour
1 teaspoon salt
100 g/4 oz (½ cup) butter
100 g/4 oz (1 cup) finely chopped walnuts
50 g/2 oz (½ cup) cut mixed (candied) peel
1 sachet (envelope) easy-blend (quick-rising) dried yeast
2 tablespoons caster (superfine) sugar
175 ml/6 fl oz (¾ cup) lukewarm milk
220 g/8 oz marzipan (almond paste)
225 g/8 oz (¾ cup) redcurrant jelly
100 g/4 oz (²/₃ cup) glacé (candied) cherries
100 g/4 oz (1 cup) icing (confectioners') sugar
a little water

Place the apricots, peaches and apple rings in a saucepan with the orange juice. Bring to the boil, then reduce the heat and simmer for 15 minutes. Set aside to cool.

Mix together the flour and salt in a bowl. Rub in (cut in) the butter, then stir in the walnuts, peel, yeast and caster (superfine) sugar. Mix in enough milk to form a fairly firm dough. Turn out the dough on to a lightly floured work surface and knead it thoroughly for 10 minutes, until it is smooth and elastic. Grease a large baking sheet or roasting pan. Roll out the dough slightly larger than 30 cm/12 in square and place it on the baking sheet. Turn up the edges slightly to form a neat rim and pinch them into an attractive, narrow border.

Drain the fruit well. Cut the marzipan (almond paste) into small pieces and dot them over the dough base. Arrange the fruit in neat rows on top, overlapping the larger pieces. Cover loosely with cling film (plastic wrap) and leave in a warm place until the dough is risen. Set the oven at 190°C/375°F/Gas 5.

Bake the kuchen for 30–40 minutes, or until the base is cooked. Melt the redcurrant jelly in a small saucepan. Arrange the cherries on the kuchen, then glaze them generously with the jelly and leave to cool. Cut the kuchen into 16 squares, leaving them all in place.

Mix the icing (confectioners') sugar with just a little water to make a thick glacé icing (frosting). Place this in a greaseproof paper (waxed paper) piping (pastry) bag and cut off just the tip of the bag. Drizzle the icing over the top of the kuchen and leave to set before removing the slices from the baking sheet.

ICE CREAM SUNDAES

These are great fun for adult or children's parties. If you are making sundaes for young children, keep the quantities small to avoid having a lot of waste. Sundaes are not really suitable for large gatherings as they have to be assembled just before they are eaten and assembling more than 12 takes too much time. Have the macerated fruit ready, and any flavoured syrup and toppings in basins with spoons to sprinkle them into glasses. Scoop the required number of dollops of ice cream onto a baking tray lined with cling film (plastic wrap) and return them to the freezer so that you do not have to do battle with this time-consuming stage at the last minute. Also have a chilled piping (pastry) bag of whipped cream ready to add the finishing touches to each sundae.

An adult sundae is a serious concoction, steeped with layers of fruit, ice cream, flavoured syrup or sauce and topped with swirls of cream and a flamboyant decoration. To treat the taste buds as well as create a vision of a feast, buy good-quality ice cream and plan the ingredients carefully.

Strawberry Sundae

Steep fresh strawberries in a little kirsch or orange-flavoured liqueur (such as Grand Marnier). Empty a jar of apricot jam into a small saucepan and add 8 tablespoons of dry sherry. Gently heat until thoroughly combined, then cool. Spoon 3 strawberries into the base of each tall glass. Top with a scoop of ice cream and trickle some of the apricot sauce over. Add 4 strawberries and some chopped toasted hazelnuts, then a couple of scoops of ice cream. Trickle more apricot sauce over, add a scoop of ice cream and several strawberries. Top with swirls of whipped cream, sprinkle with chopped hazelnuts and top with a whole strawberry.

Vanilla Sundae

Sundaes for children should be less sophisticated than those for adults. Keep the ingredients simple and top with lots of chocolate sauce. The following sundae is popular with most children.

Make a chocolate sauce: place 225 g/8 oz (8 squares) plain (semi-sweet) chocolate in a heatproof bowl with 50 g/2 oz (¼ cup) unsalted butter and 8 tablespoons of golden syrup. Place the bowl over a saucepan of barely simmering water and stir until the chocolate has completely melted. Leave to cool. Place a small scoop each of vanilla ice cream and strawberry-flavoured ice cream in a glass dish. Add a few slices of canned peaches and seedless green grapes, then top with another scoop of vanilla ice cream. Pour over a little chocolate sauce, and decorate with chocolate caraque, if liked.

Iced Tea

Make good-quality, fairly weak tea – China or Earl Grey are suitable but avoid stronger Assam or breakfast tea. Take care to ensure that the water is fresh and absolutely boiling. Allow the tea to brew (3 minutes for small-leaf tea; 5 minutes for large-leaf varieties), then strain it into a heatproof jug. Add a thin slice of lemon and a mint sprig for each cup prepared. Sweeten the tea very slightly, if liked, then add ice (one cube for each cup prepared) and leave to cool. Chill the tea before serving in Irish coffee glasses or small, slim, straight glasses. Add a

sprig of lemon balm and an ice cube to each glass, making sure there is a slice of lemon and mint sprig in each portion.

Orange Tea

Make the tea slightly weaker than you usually do. Pare the rind (peel) from an orange and infuse it with the tea and freshly boiling water, adding a cinnamon stick and 2 cloves. The rind from 1 orange is sufficient to flavour about 8 cups. Leave the tea to brew for 10 minutes (under a tea cosy to keep it hot) before straining it into warmed cups. Add halved, finely cut orange slices to the cups and serve.

Mocha Sundae

This is a delicious concoction for adults. Place 6 tablespoons of raisins in a basin and sprinkle over 4 tablespoons of brandy. Leave to soak for several hours or overnight. Make a rich chocolate sauce: place 225 g/8 oz (8 squares) plain (semi-sweet) chocolate in a heatproof basin with 50 g/2 oz (¼ cup) unsalted butter, 8 tablespoons of

golden syrup and another 4 tablespoons of brandy. Place the basin over a saucepan of hot water and stir until the chocolate has completely melted. Leave to cool. Place some chocolate sauce in the base of 6 glass dishes. Top each with 4 small scoops of coffee ice cream and sprinkle generously with chopped walnuts. Sprinkle the brandy-soaked raisins over the top, then add a scoop of coffee ice cream to each. Trickle chocolate sauce over each sundae and pipe or spoon a swirl of cream on each. Decorate with chocolate caraque, if liked.

THE COCKTAIL HOUR

Cocktails have seen something of a renaissance in recent years, and a cocktail party is one option for entertaining in the early part of the evening. If you want to indulge in the delights of dressing up, a cocktail party provides the perfect excuse for introducing a Twenties or Thirties *theme, with the women dressed as flappers and the men in black tie or wearing striped blazers.*

Carry the theme through with jazz, swing and ragtime music taped as background for the party. Food should be easy to eat with the fingers and there should be plenty of it to quell the effects of strong cocktails. On the subject of drink, make sure there are plenty of alcohol-free alternatives for those who are driving and for quenching raging thirsts before embarking on a cocktail-sampling session.

COCKTAIL STYLE

The focal point of a cocktail party is the bar. Although the kitchen is an ideal location for this, it is more fun to locate your bar in the main reception room. Here are a few pointers to bear in mind when hosting a cocktail party.

❖ Make sure you have several cocktail shakers. Have a large jug and tall mixing stick for making thirst-quenching cocktails.

❖ Lay out different shapes and sizes of glasses on separate trays ready for different strengths of mixes. Offer mineral water, fruit juices and non-alcoholic alternatives on a separate table.

❖ Place large bowls of nibbles (snacks) around the room, and make sure there are lots of canapés, or very small sandwiches, and finger food such as mini quiches and rolls with pâté.

Cocktail Checklist

- Nibbles (snacks)
- Ingredients for cocktails
- Alcohol-free drinks
- Cocktail shaker(s)
- Mixing jug
- Cocktail sticks (toothpicks)
- Ice, cubes and crushed
- Decorative cocktail umbrellas
- Cocktail garnishes (cherries, lemons, limes, etc.)
- Olives
- Cocktail glasses
- House cleaning and tidying

Offer a range of canapés, and pass them round while the guests mix.

MUSHROOM SQUARES

—————— MAKES 32 ——————

These can be filled a day ahead and chilled, ready for cooking early on the day they are served. They can, of course, be frozen ahead and they are small enough to be cooked from frozen without requiring a vast increase in cooking time.

1 tablespoon olive oil
1 small onion, finely chopped
50 g/2 oz (1/3 cup) pine kernels (nuts)
100 g/4 oz (1½ cups) button
mushrooms, chopped
4 tablespoons chopped fresh parsley
1 teaspoon chopped fresh sage
salt and freshly ground black pepper
squeeze of lemon juice
50 g/2 oz (1 cup) fresh breadcrumbs
225 g/8 oz puff pastry dough, thawed if frozen
beaten egg, to glaze

Heat the oil in a small saucepan. Add the onion and fry, stirring often, for 10 minutes, until the onion is softened but not browned. Add the pine kernels (nuts) and mushrooms and stir until the mushrooms are reduced slightly in volume and they give up their juice. Continue cooking until all the liquid has evaporated, stirring occasionally to prevent the mixture sticking to the pan. The mushroom mixture will be greatly reduced but it will have a concentrated flavour — if the liquid is not evaporated, the mixture will have a weaker flavour. Off the heat, stir in the parsley, sage, seasoning, lemon juice and breadcrumbs.

Set the oven at 220°C/425°F/Gas 7. Roll out the pastry (dough) into a 40 cm/16 in square. Cut it into 64 squares, each measuring about 5 cm/2 in. Use a teaspoon to put a little mushroom mixture on 32 pastry squares. Brush the remaining squares with a little beaten egg, then use these to cover the mushroom filling, pressing the pastry edges together neatly to seal in the filling. Place the filled pastries on an ungreased baking sheet.

Glaze the pastries with beaten egg. Bake for 12–15 minutes, until well puffed and golden brown. Transfer to a wire rack to cool. Serve hot, warm or cold.

Non-Alcoholic Cocktails

FLAMING SUNSET Half-fill a glass with sweetened cranberry juice drink. Top up with tonic or sparkling mineral water.

BITTER FRUITS Shake several dashes of bitters into a glass. Top up with chilled sparkling unsweetened white grape juice. Add a slice of lemon and a maraschino or glacé cherry on a cocktail umbrella.

MINTY MANIAC Mix peppermint cordial with a generous squeeze of lime juice and tonic. Serve in a glass with green sugar-frosted rim and float a slice of lime on top.

Frosting Glasses

The water can be tinted with a few drops of food colouring to make a coloured sugar frosting on the rim of the glass. This is a nice touch for holiday parties such as Christmas or Valentine's Day.

1 Have a saucer of caster (superfine) or granulated sugar ready. Pour a little water into a saucer. Turn a glass upside down and dip the rim straight down into the water.

2 Lift the glass cleanly upwards, then dip it straight into the sugar. Hold the glass upside down for a while.

TRAY CANAPES

MAKES ABOUT 48

Baking a large tray canapé base and piping a soft cheese topping is far easier than spending hours fiddling with small bread shapes or tiny individual pastry bases. This is an excellent way of making impressive-looking (and tasting) canapés for a large number of people, as the base can be baked the day before and the prepared topping is quickly added to the whole tray a couple of hours before serving. Choose any garnishing ingredients you like, as long as they are attractive and flavoursome.

100 g/4 oz (2 cups) fresh white breadcrumbs
50 g/2 oz (½ cup) Cheddar cheese, grated
4 tablespoons grated Parmesan cheese
2 spring onions (green onions), finely chopped
salt and freshly ground black pepper
4 eggs, separated
100 ml/4 fl oz (½ cup) milk

TOPPING
225 g/8 oz (1 cup) curd (cream) cheese
4 tablespoons mayonnaise

GARNISH
choose from: tiny smoked salmon rolls, tiny ham rolls, sliced stuffed olives, small pieces of blanched green or red pepper (sweet bell pepper), walnut halves, toasted whole blanched almonds, halved cherry tomatoes

Set the oven at 200°C/400°F/Gas 6. Line a 32.5 × 23 cm/13 × 9 in Swiss roll tin (jelly roll pan) with non-stick greaseproof paper (waxed paper).

Mix together the breadcrumbs, Cheddar, Parmesan, spring onions (green onions) and seasoning. Beat the egg yolks and milk together. In a separate, clean bowl, beat the egg whites until they stand in stiff peaks. Work fairly quickly when mixing the ingredients as the mixture stiffens on standing as the bread absorbs the moisture. Beat the egg yolk mixture into the dry ingredients, then beat in a quarter of the whisked egg whites. Using a large metal spoon, carefully fold in the remaining whites.

Turn the mixture into the lined tin (pan) and spread it out quickly and lightly. Bake at once, for 15–20 minutes, until the mixture is risen and golden.

Have a sheet of greaseproof paper (waxed paper) ready on a wire rack. Turn the baked mixture out onto the rack and carefully remove the lining paper. Leave to cool. When completely cool, return the base to the clean tin in which it was baked.

Use a sharp serrated knife to cut the baked cheese base into 4 cm/1½ in squares. Remove the corner square as this allows for easier removal of the finished canapés without disturbing the toppings.

For the topping, soften the curd (cream) cheese by stirring in the mayonnaise. Place the mixture in a piping (pastry) bag fitted with a star nozzle (tube). Pipe a small swirl of topping on each square. Top each one with a suitable garnish, pressing it gently into the soft cheese mixture. Use a small palette knife or metal spatula to remove the squares from the tray, starting in the open corner.

A Few Classic Cocktails

BLOODY MARY Mix 1 measure vodka, a dash of Worcestershire sauce, a good squeeze lemon juice, 2 measures tomato juice and add seasoning to taste.

BUCK'S FIZZ (MIMOSA) Orange juice topped up with champagne (or, for economy, dry sparkling wine) – about 1 part orange juice to 2 parts champagne.

GIN SLING Mix 2 measures gin, 1 measure cherry brandy, a squeeze of lemon juice, a twist of lemon rind (peel) and soda to top up.

MARGARITA Mix 3 measures tequila to 1 measure Cointreau. Frost the rim of the glass with lime juice and salt before pouring in the cocktail.

MARTINI Mix 1 measure gin to 1 measure dry vermouth. For a dry martini, mix 2 measures gin to 1 measure vermouth.

PIÑA COLADA Equal measures of rum, pineapple juice and coconut milk, mixed in an electric blender and served on ice.

PINK GIN Gin with a dash of Angostura Bitters and topped with tonic to taste.

Different Drink Ideas

APPLE AND BRANDY Top up brandy with unsweetened apple juice to taste. Serve with ice and a slice of lime.

CITRUS GIN Mix 2 measures gin, 2 measures orange juice, 1 measure grapefruit juice.

DAIRY MAID'S DELIGHT Mix 2 measures crème de cacao, 1 measure rum, 3 measures milk.

PASSION JUICE Mix 1 measure vodka to 3 measures passion fruit juice.

TROPICAL SUNSET Mix 1 measure vodka to 2 measures tropical fruit juice. Add a piece of pineapple, a cherry and a twist of lime on a cocktail stick or toothpick.

Not So Strong . . .

CIDER REFRESHER Mix 2 measures dry (hard) cider to 1 measure orange juice.

SPRITZER Half white wine to half sparkling mineral water (seltzer).

Cocktail Tray

Give a plain or scratched old tray a face-lift with a cut-out paper design. The instructions here show a sophisticated geometric pattern for an oval tray, but the principle can be adapted to any shape of tray. You can trim the tray just to fit it in with a particular party theme, but using strong glue and two coats of clear polyurethane varnish will effect a permanent transformation.

YOU WILL NEED: tray, paper for templates, pencil, scissors, ruler, gold and silver good-quality stiff paper, glue, black good-quality stiff paper or tape, paper or polyurethane varnish (optional).

1 For the first template, take a sheet of paper large enough to cover the base of the tray. Stand the tray on the paper and draw around the base.

2 Cut out the tray shape. Check that it fits the tray bottom accurately.

3 Fold the template in half lengthways, then open it out again. Make folds across both ends of the paper as shown, then open them out.

4 Fold the template in half again along the first fold. Fold the curved ends of the paper back towards the centre, using the second fold as a guide, then pleat the folded ends as shown to make three wedge-shaped creases at each end of the template.

5 Open out the template. Use a ruler and sharp pencil to draw lines along each of the fold marks. Draw the diamond shape and triangles in the middle of the tray. Make a second identical template.

6 Turn one template over and spread glue evenly on the unmarked side. Stick it down smoothly onto the tray so that the pencil marks are on top.

7 Fold and then cut the second template in half. You will need this quantity of gold and of silver paper, but do not yet cut out the individual segments.

8 Mark on both templates which segments are to be gold and which are to be silver: the two colours alternate.

9 Cut apart the sections of the second template, then cut out the corresponding pieces of gold and silver paper.

10 Lay the pieces of gold and silver paper in position on the tray, following the marks on the template. Check that they all fit before applying any glue.

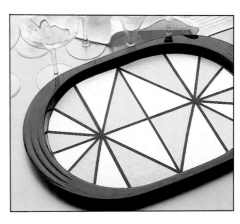

11 Glue the pieces of paper in position on the tray. (The kind of glue depends on how lasting you want the decoration to be.)

12 Cut narrow strips of black paper or tape to cover the joins between the different papers. Remember to cut the ends at angles where they join other black strips and to fit the edges of the tray neatly. Carefully glue the strips over the joins.

13 Coat the finished tray with paper varnish or two coats of clear polyurethane varnish, allowing the varnish to dry thoroughly between coats and before use.

FRIENDS FOR SUPPER

Informal suppers with people you know well are opportunities for trying new recipe ideas. Serve-yourself suppers are popular, for example, and allow guests to experiment with different flavours and textures. Table decorations can be fun, too. Experiment with different fabrics, colours and alternative centrepieces. Dispense with standard setting arrangements and give vent to individual layouts or set a completely different dining scene to reflect the chosen food.

*I*nviting friends around for an informal supper is probably one of the easiest ways of entertaining. Simple should not mean disorganized, however – it is still important to plan ahead.

SERVE-YOURSELF SUPPER
This is an easy and fun way of sharing a kitchen supper with people you know well. The numbers you can invite depends on the size of your kitchen, but you really need at least six people to make the idea worthwhile and to warrant preparing a range of foods.

Planning
The idea is to have the majority of the food prepared but to leave all the last-minute assembly to your guests. It is important to select sauces, fillings and toppings which do not deteriorate quickly on standing and to pick foods that are easy to handle. Pizza, pancakes (crêpes), baked potatoes, pasta and fritter meals are all suitable. Here are a few thoughts on planning in each case.

PIZZA Make lots of small pie bases, about 7.5 cm/3 in across so that everyone has to make up at least two or three toppings. Bake the bases in advance until they are just cooked but not browned. These may be frozen and then defrosted on the day. Lay out a

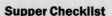

Supper Checklist
● First course
● Main course
● Dessert
● Wine
● Alcohol-free drinks
● Coffee
● Any special dietary needs?
● Table linen
● Cutlery (flatware), china and glassware
● House cleaning and tidying

wide variety of toppings and stack the pizza discs. Heat the oven and make sure you have enough baking sheets.

Prepare dips and crudités, and serve drinks while people wait for their pizza to cook. Have a salad to go with the cooked pizza.

BAKED POTATOES Bake lots of small potatoes and let guests help themselves to the toppings and fillings.

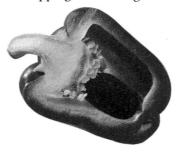

PASTA Have prepared sauces and toppings, then cook fresh pasta in front of your guests and let them help themselves to different combinations of pasta and sauces. Small bowls are best so that everyone tries a variety.

FRITTERS These can be fun: prepare a variety of suitable ingredients for making fritters, such as vegetables, seafood, cooked meat and fruit. A flour and water batter can be made in advance and whisked egg whites should be folded in at the last minute. Guests dip food into the batter, then deep-fry the pieces on fondue forks. Put out plenty of absorbent kitchen paper (paper towels) for draining the fritters and serve dipping sauces or condiments for dressing them.

Offer two or three hot fillings with a serve-yourself supper of pancakes (crêpes), such as a Light Chicken Filling (above).

PANCAKES OR CRÊPES Pancakes (crêpes) are ideal for a serve-yourself supper where a range of fillings is on offer. The pancakes can be frozen up to a couple of months ahead or they can be chilled for up to 3 days before the party. They should be well wrapped so that they don't dry out and each separated with absorbent kitchen paper (paper towels) during storage.

Stack the pancakes in ovenproof serving dishes, brush each one very lightly with a little melted butter, and cover with foil. Set the oven at 180°C/350°F/Gas 4. Reheat the pancakes about 15 minutes before everyone is ready to eat. The hot fillings should be placed on warmers or burners.

The idea is that diners serve themselves with pancakes and a little filling, then fold or roll and eat them. As well as the prepared fillings, it is a good idea to offer grated cheese, soft cheese with herbs, finely grated carrot dressed with a little French dressing, shredded cooked ham, chopped tomato and other suitable savoury ingredients so that a range of fillings can be created. Remember syrups, chocolate spread, chopped nuts and diced fresh fruit for dessert. Children love foods like frankfurters and peanut butter too!

If you want to keep the party really informal, and encourage guests to eat with their fingers, make sure all the ingredients are finely chopped so that they stay in the pancakes when wrapped, and pile stacks of good-quality paper napkins to clean sticky fingers.

LIGHT CHICKEN FILLING

——— ENOUGH TO FILL 16 PANCAKES ———
(CRÊPES) LIGHTLY

2 tablespoons oil
3 boneless chicken breasts (chicken breast
halves), skinned and cut into fine strips
salt and freshly ground black pepper
2 tablespoons chopped fresh sage
2 leeks, finely sliced
4 tablespoons flaked almonds
2 courgettes (zucchini), peeled and sliced
2 tablespoons plain (all-purpose) flour
4 tablespoons dry sherry
250 ml/8 fl oz (1 cup) chicken stock

Heat the oil in a flameproof casserole or heavy-bottomed saucepan. Add the chicken, then season well and brown the pieces all over. Sprinkle in the sage, add the leeks and almonds and continue to cook, stirring often, until the leeks are softened: about 15 minutes.

Stir in the courgettes (zucchini) and cook for 2 minutes before stirring in the flour, then pour in the sherry and stock. Bring to the boil, stirring, and reduce the heat. Simmer the mixture for 10 minutes and taste for seasoning before serving.

BASIC BATTER

——— MAKES 14—16 ———

The pancake (crêpe) batter will thicken slightly if it is left to stand for any length of time. Add a little extra water before pouring into the pan if this is the case.

100 g/4 oz (1 cup) plain (all-purpose) flour
2 eggs
300 ml/½ pint (1¼ cups) milk
1 tablespoon oil, plus extra for frying
2 tablespoons water
oil for cooking

Place the flour in a bowl and make a well in the middle. Add the eggs and a little of the milk. Gradually beat the eggs and milk together, incorporating some of the flour to make a smooth, thick batter. Gradually pour in the remaining milk until all the flour is incorporated in a smooth batter. Beat in 1 tablespoon oil and water. Leave the batter to stand for 30 minutes before cooking.

Brush a little oil over a non-stick or heavy-based flat pancake pan or frying pan (skillet). A 15—17.5 cm/6—7 in pan is best, as this makes small pancakes (crêpes) which are easy to fill and hold, and allows guests to sample all the fillings. Pour a thin layer of batter into the pan, tilting the pan to spread it evenly. Cook over a medium heat until the batter is set and the underneath lightly browned. Use a spatula or palette knife to turn the pancake and cook the second side until lightly browned. Transfer to a warm plate, cover with absorbent kitchen paper (paper towel) and continue until all the batter is used up.

Pancakes (crêpes), with Pineapple with Maple Syrup filling.

Dessert Fillings

Here are two delicious fillings for dessert pancakes (crêpes).

PINEAPPLE WITH MAPLE SYRUP Cut the base off a ripe fresh pineapple. Cut off the leafy top and the peel, making sure to remove all the spines. Cut the fruit in half and cut out the hard core in a wedge shape. Cut the fruit into small pieces and place in a bowl. Trickle pure maple syrup over. Cover and chill for at least 2 hours. Toss the pineapple in the syrup before serving. Serve with a bowl of yogurt to spoon over.

CHOCOLATE CREAM Spoon half a pot of chocolate hazelnut spread into a basin and add 2 tablespoons of brandy. Stand the basin over a saucepan of hot water and stir the chocolate mixture until it is just runny. Remove from the pan and cool slightly. Whip 300 ml/½ pint (1¼ cups) double (heavy) cream and fold it into the chocolate. Cool.

Serve-yourself Pasta

An alternative to pancakes (crêpes) – allow 100–175 g/4–6 oz (¾–1¼ cups) pasta shapes per person. Serve pasta shapes rather than noodles, which can be difficult to serve in small portions, when diners want to take several helpings to sample different toppings rather than one larger serving. Shapes are also far easier to eat with only a fork, so this is ideal for a fairly large gathering where everyone stands and chats.

❖ Dried pasta can be cooked a little ahead, tossed with a small amount of olive oil and butter, then placed in an ovenproof serving dish and covered with foil. Reheat in the oven just before serving. Cover with a lid or suitable plate to reheat in the microwave instead of the oven.

❖ Fresh pasta has to be cooked just before serving for best results but it is ready after 3 minutes' boiling. Check the manufacturers' recommended times for ready-filled pasta shapes, as they usually take a little longer.

❖ Serve some cold pasta with a variety of suitable salad vegetables and dressings. For example, offer cooked diced carrot, sweetcorn, cut green beans, green or red pepper (sweet bell pepper), diced ham, shredded salami and so on.

❖ Creamy salad dressings include yogurt with blue cheese and chives, soured cream with chopped parsley and shredded basil or fromage frais with chopped herbs and spring onions (green onions). Oil and vinegar dressing should also be included.

❖ Make fresh pesto by puréeing the leaves from a punnet of basil with pine kernels (pine nuts), freshly grated Parmesan, a couple of garlic cloves and olive oil. You need about 50 g/2 oz (⅓ cup) pine kernels, 100 g/4 oz piece of Parmesan and 250 ml/8 fl oz (1 cup) olive oil to a punnet of basil. Add seasoning to taste.

❖ Cook several chopped garlic cloves in olive oil, add plenty of freshly ground black pepper and lots of chopped parsley. Keep this warm so that it can be spooned over the pasta – it is good alone or great as a base for adding other ingredients.

Dessert Ideas for Pasta Parties

❖ Make a nutty caramelized orange salad by layering sliced fresh oranges with chopped walnuts in a heatproof dish. Coat generously with freshly made caramel and leave to cool, then chill overnight.

❖ Mix lots of diced prepared fresh and dried fruit with plain yogurt (thicker Greek-style yogurt is wonderful!). Turn it into a bowl. Roast some sesame seeds, sunflower seeds and chopped walnuts in a heavy-bottomed saucepan over low heat. Cool, then sprinkle the nut mixture and some grated chocolate over the fruit yogurt. Serve with honey, preferably the runny variety.

❖ Make a large chocolate trifle. Use chocolate cake as the base, sprinkling it with rum or brandy. Top with strawberries or raspberries and cover with custard (custard sauce). Top with a layer of whipped cream and sprinkle generously with grated chocolate. Decorate with white chocolate shapes or leaves and fresh strawberries or raspberries.

Apple Pie.

POTLUCK SUPPERS

A potluck supper where everyone brings a dish is a good idea among friends who often dine together. The host or hostess usually prepares the main course, then friends bring the first course and one or two desserts. The arrangement works well for everyone, but it is never a good idea to suggest that friends you rarely see bring some form of dish. Even a polite offer of help should not provide the excuse for off-loading your cooking onto someone else.

Quick Custard Sauce

This custard sauce is best freshly made but if you do have to make it in advance, cover the surface directly with a piece of dampened greaseproof paper (waxed paper) or cling film (plastic wrap) to prevent a skin forming.

Mix 3 tablespoons of cornflour (cornstarch) and 3 tablespoons of sugar to a paste with a little milk taken from 600 ml/1 pint (2½ cups). Stir in 3 egg yolks and a teaspoon of natural vanilla essence (extract). Carefully heat the remaining milk to just below boiling point. Remove from the heat, then gradually pour it over the cornflour mixture, stirring all the time.

Pour the custard back into the saucepan and bring to the boil, stirring all the time. Simmer for 2 minutes, then serve.

APPLE PIE

— SERVES 8 —

Serve ice cream or Quick Custard Sauce with this pie.

225 g/8 oz (2 cups) plain (all-purpose) flour
75 g/3 oz (5 tablespoons) butter
50 g/2 oz (¼ cup) white vegetable fat (shortening)
2 tablespoons water
450 g/1 lb cooking apples, peeled, cored and sliced
50 g/2 oz (⅓ cup) raisins
6 cloves
1 teaspoon ground cinnamon
75 g/3 oz (⅓ cup) caster (superfine) sugar
milk, to glaze
caster (superfine) sugar, to sprinkle

Set the oven at 190°C/375°F/Gas 5. Place the flour in a bowl, then rub in (cut in) the butter and vegetable fat (shortening). Mix in the water to bind the pastry (dough). Divide the pastry in half. Roll out half on a lightly floured surface and use to line a 23 cm/9 in tart (pie) plate.

Pile the apples in the middle of the plate, leaving the pastry on the rim uncovered. Sprinkle the raisins, cloves, cinnamon and sugar between the apple slices. Roll out the remaining pastry large enough to cover the pie completely. Dampen the pastry rim on the base of the pie, then cover it with the rolled-out pastry. Gently tuck the pastry in around the apples. Press the edges to seal them well, then trim off the excess pastry.

Knock up the pastry edges with the back of a knife, then make a small scalloped edge. Cut leaves from the pastry trimmings and arrange them on the tart. Make a small hole in the middle to allow steam to escape, then brush the pastry with milk. Bake the tart for 50–60 minutes, until the pastry is golden and the apples are well cooked.

Sprinkle caster (superfine) sugar over the tart as soon as it is removed from the oven. Serve hot or warm.

FONDUES

A fondue makes a fun, one-course feast. Even though it does not seem to be a vast quantity, do not underestimate this rich dish. Day-old French bread is best for cutting into chunks and the fondue clings to it well. A couple of light salads are always appreciated, providing guests with a palate-cleansing break between dipping sessions. Prepare a bowl of fresh

End the meal with chocolates and coffee.

fruit instead of a dessert (remember to lay out small plates and knives) or simply offer some chocolate truffles or petits fours with coffee.

Fondue Etiquette

Each diner spears the dippers on a special long-handled fondue fork and coats the food in the rich cheese dip. Regulate the burner so that the fondue is kept hot, bubbling occasionally, but not boiling.

Hidden at the bottom of the pot is the traditional delicacy which many consider to be the highlight of the meal – the golden cheese crust! Some heavy-based metal pots yield a delicious crust which comes away easily with the help of a flexible spatula.

Remember that diners who drop their dippers in the fondue have to make a forfeit – traditionally it is an occasion for kissing all the guests of the opposite sex.

A fondue is an excellent way to enjoy an informal meal with friends.

Paper Flowers Centrepiece

Choosing tissue paper in closely graded colours for these flowers achieves the vibrant, glowing quality of real live peonies or roses. You can vary the diameter of your paper circles, with 7.5 cm/3 in being about the smallest workable size.

YOU WILL NEED: tissue paper in various colours, scissors, florists' wire, darning needle (optional), green crêpe paper.

1 Cut circles of tissue paper. Fold them into quarters and flute the edges using scissors.

2 Stack four or six circles of tissue paper together. Bend a small loop in one end of a length of florists' wire. Use a needle to make a hole in the centre of the paper circles, then thread the straight end of the wire through from front to back.

3 Turn the paper over and gently bunch the circles up around the wire loop. Wind the wire around the base of the flower at the back to secure. Gently ease the tissue paper into attractive 'petal' shapes at the front.

4 Cut leaf shapes from crêpe paper in proportion to the flower heads. Although crêpe paper is stiffer than tissue, do not make them too large, or they will flop.

5 Bend small loops at one end of lengths of florists' wire and attach the leaves singly or in pairs. Arrange the finished flowers and leaves in a bowl.

SWISS CHEESE FONDUE

SERVES 4

Most fondue pans will take up to double this quantity, so you can easily multiply the recipe ingredients if you want to serve 6–8 guests. If you have a couple of spirit burners or a candle-heated table warmer which holds several candles, fondue also works well for larger numbers, particularly if you sit your guests on large cushions and arrange a couple of fondue burners on low coffee tables. Remember to ensure that the tables are sturdy to avoid accidents.

Prepare bowls of bread, thickly sliced celery, small chunks of courgette (zucchini) and small cauliflower florets (flowerets) in advance. The fondue has to be made just before it is served, so make sure all the diners are comfortable with drinks and nibbles, then warn them that you are doing to disappear to the kitchen for a little while.

450 g/1 lb (4 cups) grated Gruyère cheese
1 tablespoon plain (all-purpose) flour
salt and freshly ground black pepper
3 tablespoons freshly grated Parmesan cheese
(optional)
1 small garlic clove, crushed
150 ml/¼ pint (⅔ cup) dry white wine
2 tablespoons kirsch
grated nutmeg

Mix the Gruyère with the flour, seasoning and the Parmesan, if using. Do this well ahead and set it aside in a covered bowl.

Place the garlic in a flameproof fondue pan. For a less pronounced garlic flavour, simply rub a cut clove of garlic around the inside of the pan but do not add it to the fondue. Add the wine and heat gently until it is steaming but not boiling. Add about one-third of the cheese mixture and stir over low to medium heat until the cheese is more or less melted. Add a little more cheese and stir until it melts: continue adding the cheese in this way. Each addition should be three-quarters melted before the next batch is added. Stir the fondue all the time and regulate the heat so the cheese melts fairly quickly but the mixture does not begin to simmer.

Once all the cheese has been added, bring the fondue just to simmering point, so that it bubbles a few times, then remove the pan from the heat. Stir in the kirsch and nutmeg to taste. Transfer the fondue pot to a spirit burner.

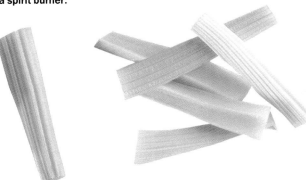

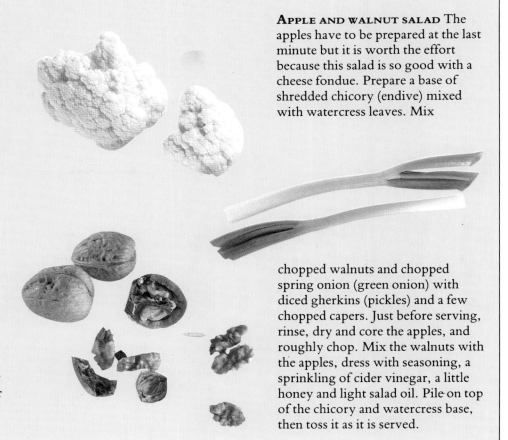

Side Dishes for Fondue

BASIL-DRESSED TOMATO SALAD
The combination of tomato and fresh basil is a particularly delicious one, and it is excellent to go with a cheese dish. Peel ripe tomatoes, remove their cores and cut them into eighths, which are easier to eat using just a fork than when sliced. Sprinkle with a little caster

(superfine) sugar and seasoning. Dress with plenty of shredded basil leaves and trickle a little olive oil over. Add a squeeze of lemon juice and sprinkle with snipped chives. Leave to marinate for at least 1 hour before serving: the salad will last for 2–3 hours in the marinade without becoming too soggy.

APPLE AND WALNUT SALAD The apples have to be prepared at the last minute but it is worth the effort because this salad is so good with a cheese fondue. Prepare a base of shredded chicory (endive) mixed with watercress leaves. Mix

chopped walnuts and chopped spring onion (green onion) with diced gherkins (pickles) and a few chopped capers. Just before serving, rinse, dry and core the apples, and roughly chop. Mix the walnuts with the apples, dress with seasoning, a sprinkling of cider vinegar, a little honey and light salad oil. Pile on top of the chicory and watercress base, then toss it as it is served.

Bowl of Candles

Make a bowl of candles for the centrepiece of an informal supper party. Use a bowl which has a lovely rim or highly decorated exterior. Colourful stones or coloured glass pebbles could also be used to cover the sand.

YOU WILL NEED: a suitable bowl, sand, coloured candles in different sizes, a range of sea shells.

1 Fill the bowl two-thirds full with clean sand. The sand must be deep enough to support the candles. Place a tall candle securely in the middle of the bowl.

2 Place shorter candles around the central candle. Depending on the size of the bowl, you may have room for several rows of candles, with each row getting smaller towards the edge of the bowl.

3 Once the candles are in position, arrange a variety of pretty shells around them to cover the sand completely.

Winter Candles

This seasonal arrangement of pine cones and nuts can be transformed into a Christmas centrepiece with a coating of gold or silver spray paint. Tie a gold or silver ribbon around the outer rim of the bowl and finish with a bow.

YOU WILL NEED: a suitable bowl, sand, candles of different sizes, pine cones, selection of nuts.

NOTE: Never leave candles unattended and make sure they do not burn down too close to any decorative arrangements.

1 Fill the bowl two-thirds full with clean sand. The sand must be deep enough to support the candles. Place a tall candle in the middle of the bowl, and arrange smaller ones around it.

2 Once the candles are in position, arrange the pine cones on the sand.

3 Fill any gaps left by the pine cones on the sand with nuts.

DINING IN STYLE

*P*roper dinner parties can be fun, as well as formal, especially if you know your guests well. This is an opportunity to lay the table with your best table linen and chinaware, and to prepare dishes that are special and out of the ordinary. Plan to have all the cooking calmly under control and to allow yourself a period of all-important relaxation before your guests arrive so you are on sparkling form and can enjoy the occasion.

GIVING A DINNER PARTY

This is an occasion when you will probably want to impress your guests – especially if the boss or important business contacts are coming for dinner. To ensure everything goes smoothly, draw up a checklist of things that need to be done, starting with jobs that can easily be completed a few days before the event, such as the shopping and cleaning. Try to prepare as much as possible in advance: make and freeze suitable dishes – dishes that can't be frozen can be made the day before and stored in the refrigerator. Leave only the finishing touches to be done on the day. One word of warning – as a general rule don't be tempted to try out a dish you've never cooked before and avoid preparing anything too complicated, particularly when you don't know your guests well and it's important that the evening is a success. You'll feel more confident offering a tried-and-tested favourite – remember, it will be new to your dinner guests – than possibly struggling with an unknown dish that is not turning out as expected. And you certainly don't want to spend most of the evening in the kitchen!

Menu Reminders

Menus for dinner parties are best kept simple, and cook-ahead dishes are ideal, as most will not spoil if your guests linger over pre-dinner drinks.
❖ Simple first courses often make the most memorable appetizers – opt for prime-quality ingredients and serve them with style. You might try avocados and chopped walnuts with a oil and vinegar dressing, melon with Parma ham (*prosciutto*) or fresh figs (serve with a twist of freshly ground black pepper), or juicy melon balls with ginger and a little mint.

❖ Classic casseroles such as Coq au Vin, Boeuf Bourguignon or a rich Hungarian goulash are practical and versatile dinner party fare. Lightly spiced curries are also most acceptable and they often benefit from being cooked a day ahead.
❖ Even if you plan an elaborate dessert, it is a good idea to offer a simple alternative. Do not dismiss fresh fruit – turn out a salad of exotic fruit or a platter of prepared mango slices, pineapple slices, halved passion fruit and sliced figs. Sorbets (water ice), meringues with whipped cream or a rich chocolate mousse are all favourites.

Opposite: a dinner party table set for a special occasion. An arrangement of fresh flowers completes the picture.

Dinner Party Checklist

- Pre-dinner drinks
- Pre-dinner nibbles (snacks)
- First course
- Main course
- Dessert
- Cheese and biscuits (crackers), fruit
- Coffee
- Brandy and liqueurs
- Any special dietary needs?
- Table linen
- Cutlery (flatware), china and glassware
- Flowers
- House cleaning and tidying

CHICKEN KORMA

—————— SERVES 4 ——————

A lightly spiced creamy dish which is ideal for serving at a dinner party. It is an ideal dish to cook ahead.

75 g/3 oz (⅓ cup) ghee or clarified butter
2 onions
2 garlic cloves, crushed
3 tablespoons grated fresh root ginger
1 tablespoon ground coriander
1 teaspoon ground cumin
2 cloves
4 green cardamom pods
1 cinnamon stick
1 bay leaf
6 boneless chicken breasts (chicken breast halves), skinned and cut into chunks
250 ml/8 fl oz (1 cup) plain yogurt
2 tablespoons ground almonds
1 tablespoon rose water
100 ml/4 fl oz (½ cup) water
salt and freshly ground black pepper
50 g/2 oz (½ cup) slivered almonds
250 ml/8 fl oz (1 cup) single (light) cream
chopped fresh coriander leaves (cilantro), to garnish

Heat a third of the ghee or butter in a frying pan (skillet). Chop 1 onion finely and add it to the ghee with the garlic and ginger. Cook, stirring often, for 10 minutes, then stir in the coriander, cumin, cloves, cardamom pods, cinnamon and bay leaf. Cook the spices for about 5 minutes, stirring all the time. Remove from the heat and cool slightly. Place the chicken in a basin and pour the cooked onion mixture over. Add the yogurt, mix well, cover and chill overnight.

Heat half the remaining ghee or butter in a flameproof casserole. Use a slotted spoon to lift the chicken from the yogurt marinade, draining off as much of the yogurt as possible, then add the pieces to the pan and brown them lightly. Stir in the ground almonds and cook for

2 minutes, then add the yogurt marinade, scraping all the spices from the basin, and the rose water. Pour in the water and add plenty of seasoning. Stir until the mixture begins to simmer, then cover the pan and leave the chicken to cook gently for 45 minutes.

Meanwhile, roast the slivered almonds in a heavy-based frying pan (skillet), stirring them virtually all the time, until they are golden brown. Tip the almonds out of the pan, add the remaining ghee or butter to the pan, thinly slice the remaining onion and brown the slices.

Stir the cream into the korma, then heat gently without boiling and taste for seasoning. Serve topped with the browned onions, roasted almonds and a sprinkling of chopped coriander leaves (cilantro).

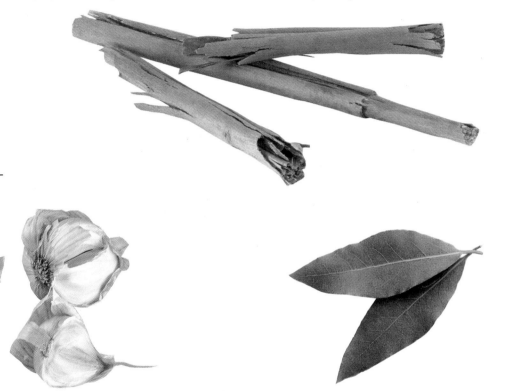

Opposite: Chicken Korma with Saffron Pilau Rice, Spiced Spinach and Mushroom Bhaji.

CHICKEN KORMA: SIDE DISHES

Saffron Pilau Rice
This savoury rice is the perfect accompaniment to Chicken Korma. Cook a chopped onion, 3 green cardamom pods, a bay leaf, a cinnamon stick and 4 cloves in 25 g/1 oz (2 tablespoons) butter. Wash 225 g/8 oz (1½ cups) basmati rice in cold water and drain before adding to the pan. Pour in 600 ml/1 pint (2½ cups) cold water and add seasoning. Bring to the boil, stir once, then cover the pan tightly and reduce the heat to the minimum. Leave to simmer for 20 minutes. Meanwhile, pound a teaspoon of saffron strands to a powder in a mortar, using a pestle. Add 2 tablespoons of boiling water and

stir well. Cook a sliced onion in some butter until browned, add a tablespoon of cumin seeds and cook for 2 minutes. Sprinkle the saffron over the rice, cover the pan quickly and leave for 5 minutes. Fork the rice into a serving dish and top with the browned onions and cumin.

Spiced Spinach
Spiced spinach is a typical side dish for many curried main courses. Trim and thoroughly wash 1 kg/2 lb fresh spinach. Cook a chopped onion, a crushed garlic clove, a teaspoon of turmeric and 2 tablespoons of cumin seeds in a little ghee, butter or oil. Add the spinach and cover the pan tightly, then cook for 5 minutes, shaking the

pan often. Uncover and continue to cook for another 5 minutes, or until the liquid has evaporated and the spinach is tender. Season to taste.

Mushroom Bhaji
Cook a chopped onion in 25 g/1 oz (2 tablespoons) butter until soft. Add a bay leaf, 2 teaspoons of ground coriander, a quarter teaspoon of grated nutmeg, a pinch of chilli powder and 450 g/1 lb sliced mushrooms. Cook, stirring occasionally, for 30 minutes, until the liquor from the mushrooms has evaporated. Stir in a 400 g/14 oz can of chopped tomatoes and season to taste, then simmer for 10 minutes. Sprinkle with chopped fresh coriander leaves (cilantro) before serving.

Seafood Surprise.

SEAFOOD SURPRISE

SERVES 6

The simple filling in this pastry seafood dish
makes for quick and easy preparation.

175 g/6 oz peeled cooked prawns (shrimp)
150 g/5 oz packet soft cheese with herbs
and garlic
1 tablespoon chopped fresh tarragon (optional)
1 × 175 g/6 oz can crab meat, drained
225 g/8 oz puff pastry dough, thawed if frozen
8 small trout fillets, or 4 large trout fillets,
skinned
salt and freshly ground black pepper
beaten egg, to glaze
sprig of fresh tarragon, to garnish

Set the oven at 220°C/425°F/Gas 7. Grease a
baking sheet. Mix the prawns (shrimp) with the
soft cheese and tarragon, if using. Lightly mix
in the crab meat. The seasoning from the
cheese should be sufficient to flavour the
mixture.

Cut the pastry (dough) in half, one portion
slightly larger than the other. Roll out the
smaller portion into an oblong measuring 30 ×
12.5 cm/12 × 5 in. Place on the baking sheet.
Top with the trout fillets, leaving a border
around the edge of the pastry and overlapping
the fillets as necessary. Season the fillets
lightly, then top with the prawn and crab
mixture.

Roll out the second sheet of pastry slightly
larger, so it will cover the filling. Fold the pastry
in half lengthways, then use a sharp serrated
knife to make cuts into the folded edge. Start
5 cm/2 in away from the end and make the cuts
at 2.5 cm/1 in intervals, leaving the last

5 cm/2 in without cuts. Cut about two-thirds
of the way across the pastry.

Brush the pastry border around the fish with
a little beaten egg. Lift the folded pastry over
the filling, so the fold runs down the middle of
the filling, then open out the pastry to cover the
filling completely. The cuts should appear as
slits down the length of the pastry lid. Press the
edges of the pastry together well to seal in the
filling. Use the blunt side of a knife to knock up
the pastry edges, then flute them into an
attractive border. Brush the pastry with beaten
egg. Bake for 15 minutes. Reduce the oven
temperature to 200°C/400°F/Gas 6 without
opening the oven door and continue baking for
a further 15–20 minutes, until the pastry is
well puffed and golden and the filling cooked
through. Garnish with a sprig of tarragon and
serve at once.

PINEAPPLE AND LIME CHEESECAKE

——— SERVES 6 ———

An unusual method that turns out a perfect cheesecake with zesty, exotic flavours.

*100 g/4 oz chocolate digestive biscuits,
crushed*
50 g/2 oz (¼ cup) unsalted butter, melted
50 g/2 oz (½ cup) cornflour (cornstarch)
grated rind (peel) of ½ lime
50 ml/2 fl oz (¼ cup) lime juice
50 g/2 oz (¼ cup) caster (superfine) sugar
1 × 200 g/7 oz can crushed pineapple
1 egg, separated
225 g/8 oz (1 cup) cream cheese
*225 g/8 oz (1 cup) curd (cream) cheese or
low-fat soft cheese*

DECORATION
strips of lemon rind (peel)
strips of lime rind (peel)
2 teaspoons caster (superfine) sugar
150 ml/¼ pint (⅔ cup) double (heavy) cream

Mix the biscuits with the butter and press the mixture into the base of a 25 cm/10 in round, loose-bottomed cake tin (pan). Chill the biscuit mixture until firm.

In a heavy-bottomed or non-stick saucepan, mix the cornflour (cornstarch) with the lime rind (peel), juice and sugar to make a smooth paste. Stir in the can of pineapple with all its juice. Stir the mixture over low to medium heat until it boils, then simmer for 3 minutes. The mixture makes a thick fruit sauce which must be stirred all the time to prevent lumps forming. Remove the pan from the heat and stir in the egg yolk, then quickly beat in the cream cheese until it is evenly distributed. Beat in the curd (cream) cheese, making sure it is evenly distributed. The mixture must not have any lumps of cheese in it.

Whisk the egg white until it stands in stiff but not dry peaks, then fold it into the cheese mixture. Pour the cheese mixture over the biscuit base, spreading it evenly. Chill the cheesecake overnight.

Pineapple and Lime Cheesecake.

Whip the cream until it stands in soft peaks, then spoon it into a piping (pastry) bag fitted with a star nozzle (tube). Remove the cheesecake from the tin and place it on a flat platter – a large cake stand is ideal. Pipe cream around the edge of the cheesecake. Toss the strips of rind (peel) in the sugar and decorate the piped cream.

Chocolate Mint Hearts

These Chocolate Mint Hearts are excellent for serving at the end of special meals. Mix 100 g/4 oz (½ cup) cream cheese with 2 tablespoons of icing (confectioners') sugar and a few drops of peppermint essence (extract). You can add a hint of green food colouring if you like. Melt 225 g/8 oz plain (semi-sweet) chocolate in a bowl placed over a pan of hot water. Lay a sheet of baking parchment on a baking sheet.

Spread half the chocolate on the paper into a square measuring about 17.5 cm/7 in. Chill the chocolate quickly in the freezer so it sets, then spread the cream cheese mixture over it and chill for 10 minutes longer. Do not leave the remaining chocolate over hot water while you do this or it will overheat and separate. Instead, warm the chocolate again just before you are ready to use it. Spread the remaining chocolate over the cheese mixture. Leave at room temperature until only just set – do not chill.

Use a heart-shaped aspic cutter to stamp out hearts in the mixture. Dip the cutter in hot water and wipe it with kitchen paper (paper towel) after each cut. Now chill the hearts without removing them from the paper. When thoroughly set, invert on to the work surface, carefully peel back the paper away from the mints and trim off the spare scraps to free the hearts. The underside, on the paper, will be shiny – lift the chocolate hearts carefully with a palette knife (metal spatula) to avoid handling and marking them.

Ribbon Candle Holder Trims

Simple and quick to conjure up, these pretty ribbon trims can be made to echo a special colour scheme. Remember: lit candles should never be left unattended, and make sure they do not burn to within reach of the candle holder trims.

YOU WILL NEED: wide-topped candle holders, fine garden or florists' wire, ribbon, scissors, candles, herbs or other greenery (optional).

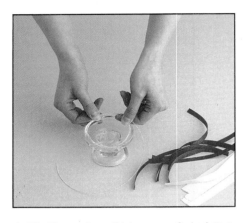

1 Wind two or three thicknesses of wire into a ring just large enough to fit neatly inside the top of each candle holder. Twist the ends of the wire around the ring to secure.

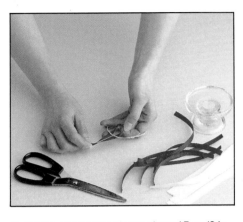

2 Cut the ribbon into pieces about 15 cm/6 in long. Double a length of ribbon and insert the loop under the wire.

3 Pass the ends of the ribbon through the loop and tighten to knot it on the wire.

4 Continue knotting ribbon around the wire ring until the wire is completely covered.

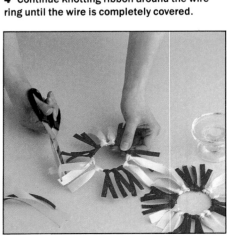

5 Trim the ends of the ribbon to neaten, then repeat for the second ring. Place the wire rings in the candle holders. Decorate with herbs or other greenery if wished.

Valentine's Heart

Set hearts a-flutter with this red and white ribbon-covered decoration. Choose ribbons in pattern variations on your chosen colour scheme. Alternatively, use patterned and plain fabric, carefully cut into ribbon strips.

YOU WILL NEED: 50–60 cm/20–24 in thick plastic-covered garden wire, piece of florists' wire, about 7.5 m/8 yd ribbon 2.5 cm/1 in wide, about 0.5 m/½ yd ribbon 5 cm/2 in wide, scissors, needle and thread.

1 Twist the thick wire into a heart shape and bind the two ends together securely in the centre with florists' wire. Cut the narrower ribbon into approximately 15 cm/6 in lengths.

2 Double a length of ribbon and knot it over the wire. Repeat with more ribbon knots until the wire is completely covered.

3 Fold a 20 cm/8 in length of wider ribbon to make a bow loop and hold it together with a couple of stitches.

4 Loop the rest of the wider ribbon around the middle of the bow loop and shape into a pair of tails. Secure with a stitch or two.

5 Attach the bow at the centre of the heart to cover the florists' wire. Trim the ends of the ribbon into swallowtail shapes.

Valentine's Day Dinner Party

❖ Cut heart-shaped invitations and send them to good friends who will want to share Valentine's Day night as a foursome.

❖ The menu is light and pink champagne is the perfect drink!

❖ The idea of the menu is that it can be romantic for two, or something of a fun occasion for four. Take the "pink heart" theme to extremes by fixing a pink cocktail before dinner – a mixture of Angostura Bitters, gin and tonic. It can be fun to go completely over the top by preparing heart-shaped cheese biscuits (crackers) too!

STYLISH BUFFETS

Preparing a buffet is the practical answer to most types of home entertaining when more than eight people are invited. The buffet can, of course, be equally as impressive as a sit-down menu, as this section highlights.

There are a few brief reminders on the important points of

planning with a few hints on pitfalls to avoid. The food really does command attention at a buffet, but to complement a glorious spread make sure you dress up the table with swags or garlands and generous bows of ribbon. Flowers may form the backdrop or centrepiece, or a fantastic pyramid arrangement of exotic fruit will definitely steal the show.

Lastly, don't hide your buffet away, let guests absorb the beauty of your art before the meal – throw open the dining room doors and allow a sense of anticipation to prevail.

BUFFET BANQUETS

❖ Site the buffet in a cool, well ventilated place: away from radiators and out of the sun.

❖ Cover the table with a protective cloth before adding the decorative linen as there are always spills when guests serve themselves.

❖ The buffet should be set with savoury food for the main part of the meal. If a starter (appetizer) is served it can be brought to the buffet at the beginning of the meal where the hostess should assist the guests with it. Alternatively, and the better arrangement, the first course should be served from a side table.

❖ Desserts and cheese may be served from the buffet if the main dishes are removed. If, at large gatherings, the desserts and cheese are set out before the main course is cleared, then a side table should be prepared for them.

❖ If port or red wine is served with cheese at small gatherings, then it may be served from the buffet rather than the bar.

❖ Always make arrangements for receiving used dishes and cutlery (flatware) when preparing a buffet. At a large gathering some guests may not feel inclined to bring their dishes out to the kitchen, therefore it is a good idea to set up a trolley (cart) where these may be placed if you have not hired a waitress or waiter to remove them.

Buffet Checklist

- Invitations
- Contact caterers, if using
- Organize serving staff, if using
- Pre-buffet nibbles (snacks)
- First course
- Main course
- Dessert
- Cheese and biscuits (crackers), fruit
- Wines
- Alcohol-free drinks
- Ice
- Coffee
- Brandy and liqueurs
- Any special dietary needs?
- Table linen
- Cutlery (flatware) – in napkin or separate
- China and glassware
- Flowers
- House cleaning and tidying

Avoiding Buffet Pitfalls

❖ Have dishes which are easy to serve – complicated dishes may make guests feel inhibited about attempting to help themselves.

❖ Avoid offering foods which really must be cut with a knife for easy eating.

❖ Avoid putting a first course on the buffet with all the main dishes so that everyone advances on all the food at once: if you want to keep a dish as a first course, then make sure you serve it yourself, otherwise guests will pile on the salads and other food, too.

❖ Arrange savoury and sweet foods on dishes at different levels, rather than in flat dishes and two or three rows deep on the table. Use cake stands and stemmed dishes to full advantage so the food creates a splendid display.

❖ Serve salad dressing separately for guests to help themselves, otherwise you may have lots of dressed salad which has to be thrown out.

A fine selection of cheeses for the buffet table is always welcome.

COUSCOUS WITH PEPPERS

—————— SERVES 8—10 ——————

This is an excellent side dish for a buffet.

6 tablespoons olive oil
2 garlic cloves, crushed
2 large onions, chopped
1 teaspoon dried oregano
2 green peppers (sweet bell peppers), seeded and diced
2 red peppers (sweet bell peppers), seeded and diced
2 yellow peppers (sweet bell peppers), seeded and diced
450 g/1 lb tomatoes, peeled, quartered and seeded
salt and freshly ground black pepper
450 g/1 lb couscous
75 g/3 oz (5 tablespoons) butter
100 g/4 oz (3/4 cup) black (ripe) olives, stoned (pitted) and thinly sliced
4 tablespoons chopped fresh parsley, (optional)
fresh sprigs of parsley, to garnish

Heat the oil in a heavy-based saucepan. Add the garlic, onions and oregano, then cook, stirring often, for 20 minutes, until the onions are softened but not browned. Add all the peppers and cook, stirring often, for a further 15 minutes. Stir in the tomatoes and seasoning, cover and simmer for 15 minutes.

Meanwhile, place the couscous in a large heatproof bowl. Pour boiling water over it to cover the grains by about 2.5cm/1 in. Cover the bowl with a plate and leave to stand for 15—20

minutes by which time the couscous will be fluffy and hot, ready to serve. The couscous may be prepared in advance by covering with cold water, then heated briefly in the microwave at the last minute.

Melt the butter in a saucepan, then pour it over the couscous and fork it into the grains. Tip the couscous into a serving bowl. Add the olives and chopped parsley, if liked, to the pepper mixture, then pour it over the couscous. Garnish with fresh sprigs of parsley and serve.

GALANTINE OF CHICKEN

—————— SERVES 8—12 ——————

A galantine of chicken can be prepared and frozen up to one month ahead of the party, ready for thawing and roasting the day before it is served. Alternatively, simply prepare and roast it the day before, cooling it quickly and chilling it overnight. A butcher or supermarket poultry counter will bone out the bird, as long as you order it in advance.

1.6 kg/3½ lb chicken, boned

STUFFING
450 g/1 lb (2 cups) medium-fat soft cheese, such as Philadelphia Light
100 g/4 oz (2 cups) fresh white breadcrumbs
1 tablespoon chopped fresh sage
4 large spring onions (green onions), finely chopped
salt and freshly ground black pepper
100 g/4 oz (3/4 cup) shelled and roughly chopped lightly salted pistachio nuts
4—6 large slices good-quality cooked ham, trimmed of fat

GARNISH
salad ingredients
herb sprigs

Set the oven at 180°C/350°F/Gas 4. Mix the soft cheese with the breadcrumbs, sage, spring onions (green onions) and plenty of seasoning. Add the nuts and pound the ingredients together well. This stuffing must not be too soft but it should be of a suitable consistency for pressing evenly on to the chicken.

Lay the chicken on a board, with the skin down. Spread one-third of the filling over the middle of the bird, then top with half the cooked ham, overlapping the slices neatly. Distribute half the remaining stuffing over the top without disrupting the base layers. Top with the remaining ham, then add the rest of the stuffing. Fold the sides of the chicken over and sew it up to enclose the filling completely.

Turn the chicken over and place it on a sheet of well-greased foil. Plump up the chicken into a neat shape, then close the foil around it, sealing the edges well. Place in a roasting pan and cook for 1½ hours. Open the foil and cook for a further 15—20 minutes to brown the top of the bird. Close the foil again and leave the chicken to cool in the baking juices, then chill it for at least 2 hours before slicing the galantine.

Use a sharp serrated knife to slice the chicken and arrange the slices on a serving platter. Garnish with salad ingredients and/or fresh herbs. Alternatively, the chicken may be coated with a classic chaudfroid sauce.

COOK'S TIP
As for most other buffet foods, the number of servings you can expect a recipe to yield depends on the number of guests and size of the buffet. If this size galantine is served as the only main dish, with a small selection of side salads, then it will comfortably serve 8 persons. Two or more galantines will serve at least 12, if not 15.

Stuffings for Galantines

The type of stuffing you use to stuff a boned bird influences the number of portions which the galantine will yield. The soft cheese and ham stuffing in the main recipe gives a plump galantine which slices well when cold, so each slice is a generous portion. Richer stuffings may be used in smaller quantities and the bird rolled rather than plumped up, which will result in smaller slices and fewer portions. A rich pâté, for example, makes an excellent filling, either on its own or spread over slices of cooked ham, which are then rolled before being placed in the boned bird. Alternatively, try a sage and onion stuffing with sausage meat.

Opposite: Couscous with Peppers.

FROZEN CHOCOLATE TERRINE

—— SERVES 12 ——

Frozen Chocolate Terrine keeps for up to one month in the freezer if the tin (pan) is well wrapped in a plastic freezer bag once the chocolate mixture has frozen solid.

450 g/1 lb (16 squares) plain (semi-sweet) chocolate
175 g/6 oz (¾ cup) unsalted butter
4 tablespoons brandy
6 eggs
225 g/8 oz (8 squares) white chocolate
150 ml/¼ pint (⅔ cup) whipping (heavy) cream

DECORATION
50 g/2 oz (2 squares) white chocolate
frosted decorations such as crystallized violets
small frosted mint leaves

Line the base of a 1.8 litre/3 pint (7½ cup) loaf tin (pan) with non-stick baking parchment. Place the plain (semi-sweet) chocolate, three-quarters of the butter, the brandy and 4 egg yolks in a heatproof bowl. Place the bowl over a saucepan of hot but not boiling water – the pan should be smaller than the base of the bowl to prevent any moisture reaching the chocolate mixture. Stir the chocolate mixture until melted and smooth.

Remove the bowl of chocolate from the saucepan. Beat 4 egg whites until they stand in stiff peaks but are not dry in texture. Stir 1 spoonful of the whites into the chocolate, then use a large metal spoon to fold in the remaining whites. Spoon the mixture into the tin and place it in the freezer for 40 minutes.

Meanwhile, place the white chocolate and remaining butter and egg yolks in a heatproof bowl and melt like the dark chocolate mixture. Whip the cream until it holds its shape in soft peaks. Stir 1 spoonful of the cream into the chocolate, then use a large metal spoon to fold in the rest of the cream. Beat the remaining egg whites until still stiff but not dry and fold them into the white chocolate mixture. Turn the white chocolate mixture into the tin on top of the dark chocolate. Freeze until firm. Seal in a freezerproof plastic bag; return to the freezer.

To serve the terrine, select a large, flat freezerproof platter. Dip the base of the tin in a bowl of very hot water and dry the outside quickly with a towel. Slide a knife around the inside of the tin to loosen the mixture, cover with the platter and invert both, giving a firm shake. Lift the tin off and remove the lining paper. Return to the freezer.

Melt the white chocolate for decoration as above. Spoon it into a small greaseproof paper (waxed paper) piping (pastry) bag and fold the ends over to seal in the chocolate. When you are ready to pipe the chocolate, snip off just the tip of the paper bag. Pipe chocolate from side to side across the top of the terrine, creating a zig-zag pattern along the whole length. Return the terrine to the freezer until it is to be taken to the buffet table. Add crystal-lized violets and tiny sugar-frosted mint leaves to complete the decoration just before serving the terrine. Use a sharp serrated knife, dipped in a jug (pitcher) of very hot water, to slice the terrine. Wipe the knife after cutting each slice.

For a more substantial cheeseboard, offer bunches of grapes and bowls of nuts and olives.

THE ULTIMATE CHEESEBOARD

Whether the cheese course is an adjunct to the meal or an important feature of the buffet is entirely up to you. Some of the finest buffet parties are those that rely totally on cheese – a really good cheese and wine party is not to be dismissed; however, avoid the Sixties-style approach of having tiny cubes of anonymous cheese speared on cocktail sticks (toothpicks). Here are some thoughts on the types of cheeses to offer and on the various ways that they can be presented.

Selection for the Cheese Course

A European practice is to serve a limited variety of cheeses as a first course, a course before dessert or as an alternative to dessert or at the end of the meal. Decide on three to six types of cheese, including hard cheeses, blue

Offer a separate cheeseboard of soft cheeses.

cheeses and soft-rind cheeses. Because this cheese selection is intended to complement the other foods on the buffet – or after a formal meal – it is best to avoid the heavily seasoned cheeses, such as those with strong herbs, garlic, nuts or chutneys blended into them. Present the soft cheese on one platter, the hard types on another, or use the same platter with separate knives for both types. Grapes or fresh dates are usually offered together with plain biscuits (crackers).

A Special Cheese Dish

This replaces the cheeseboard and it is served as a course before or after dessert, again in the European style. It is an ideal dish to replace dessert. Potted cheese is suitable. For example, pound blue Stilton to a paste with a little unsalted butter and some port, then press it into a pot and chill lightly. Cheddar can be potted the same way with a little butter, mustard and cider (hard cider).

For a more sophisticated and lighter-flavoured alternative, try a brandied Brie. Scrape the rind from 225 g/8 oz ripe brie and cut the cheese into pieces. Soak in 2 tablespoons of brandy for several hours, then mash well. Mix with 75 g/3 oz (1½ cups) fresh white breadcrumbs and 3–4 tablespoons of single (light) cream. Place the mixture in a serving dish and chill well before serving with biscuits (crackers).

Wide Variety of Cheese

Cheese may be included as part of a mixed buffet to be eaten at any stage, rather than as a separate course. For example, cheese may be eaten with a salad accompaniment. In this case, offer several different types of cheese and group them on platters. Arrange semi-soft and soft cheeses, such as Brie and Camembert, together with soft-rinded goats' cheese and pots of cream cheese flavoured with herbs. Garnish the cheeses with grapes, dates and figs.

❖ Arrange a selection of hard cheeses on a board, such as Cheddar, Jarlsberg, Gruyère and so on. Blue cheeses may be included on this platter, or simply offer one excellent piece of blue cheese on a dish by itself. Use plenty of crisp celery sticks and leaves to garnish the hard cheeseboard.

❖ A third platter may include flavoured cheeses – hard cheeses to which chives, garlic, nuts, onion or herbs have been added. Pepper-coated cheeses and flavoured soft cheeses may also be included.

Serving a Single Cheese

Offering one popular cheese in prime condition is an economical and sophisticated option. A small whole Brie or slice of a whole Stilton are both ideal. To do this well you must check the quality and ripeness of the cheese before buying it. A specialist cheese

Wrap eating utensils prettily in a napkin.

merchant or good delicatessen is the ideal place to order the cheese a couple of weeks in advance. Alternatively, speak to the delicatessen manager at the supermarket a week before the party to check the availability of whole cheeses and their ripeness.

A Cheese and Wine Party

If you are going to do this, do it well! Do not be tempted to let lots of alternative side dishes and salads creep into the menu: stick to an excellent selection of cheeses, with one cheese recipe, such as a brandied Brie, fruit and a single salad.

❖ Arrange different types of cheeses on separate platters.

❖ Offer a good choice of plain biscuits (crackers) and crispbreads, crusty bread, wholemeal (whole-wheat) and rye breads.

❖ Serve marinated cheeses in attractive, colourful bowls to indicate their colourful flavours. For example, marinate feta cheese cubes in olive oil, garlic and chopped herbs. Or marinate small whole cheeses, such as goats' cheeses, in a mixture of salad oil and walnut oil, with basil, chopped black (ripe) olives and sun-dried tomatoes.

❖ Serve a platter of different goats' cheeses with fresh figs and dates.

❖ Bowls of olives, small pickles or silverskin onions and gherkins (pickles) should be arranged around the table.

❖ A simple, green salad, with dressing offered separately, is excellent for refreshing the palate. Do not make mixed salads and creamy dressings which confuse the menu.

❖ Include bowls of fruit, positioning them near the cheeses they complement; for example, have a deep dish of polished apples near the hard cheese and a basket of pears on tissue paper for the soft cheeses.

❖ Make a vegetable arrangement from celery, radishes, carrot sticks, cauliflower florets (flowerets) and chicory (endive) leaves as a centrepiece for the table. Include fresh vine (grape) leaves if available and herb sprigs.

❖ Include a selection of nuts. A bowl of nuts in their shells looks attractive – remember the nut crackers – but an arrangement of shelled nuts on a large platter is more practical. Have both – a shallow dish of shelled nuts on a huge flat basket looks brilliant surrounded with an arrangement of nuts in shells.

INDEX